MW00948441

Higher Love
The Miraculous Story of a Family

Allison and Julie —

Love make a family!

Thanks for your support!

Randy
and
Paul

Higher Love
The Miraculous Story of a Family

PAUL CAMPION and RANDY JOHNSON

with BOBBI BUCHANAN

Ginkgo Leaf Press
2016

Authors' note: The events described in this book are real and recalled to the best of our ability. While we present this story as our truth, we also recognize that it is our perspective and may vary from the perspective of others. In some cases, the names of individuals and identifying characteristics have been changed to maintain anonymity.

First Printing: 2016

ISBN 978-1-365-00607-4

Ginkgo Leaf Press
100 Rosemont Street
Somerset, Kentucky 42503
www.higherlovebook.com

Front cover photographs by William Kolb
Cover design by Becky Tiller

Ordering Information:

Special discounts are available on quantity purchases by corporations, associations, educators, and others. For details, email higherlovebook@gmail.com.

U.S. trade bookstores and wholesalers: Please email higherlovebook@gmail.com

Dedication

To our children's birthmothers, Teresa, Sally, and April, who made our dreams of parenting come true.

To our four children, Tevin, Tyler, DeSean, and Mackenzie, who have made our lives complete.

Contents

Introduction

I hadn't seen Randy in the flesh for almost thirty years when I met him and Paul at Heine Brothers one Sunday afternoon in August 2014 to chat about their idea for a memoir.

I'd lost touch with Randy after moving away from the rich rolling hills and fertile farm fields of southern Bullitt County, Kentucky, to attend college in Lexington. But my mother and oldest sister, Mary, who ran a beauty salon just a few miles from our old stomping grounds in Belmont, kept me apprised of our former neighborhood's affairs. My mother ran a tanning bed out of Mary's shop, and despite her strict Catholic upbringing and her highly vocal opposition to homosexuality, she loved Randy from his days at the church we all attended together and was delighted when he and Paul showed up for their appointments with their newly adopted African-American infants. Like many holding fast to religious convictions, my mother could not accept the fact that people were born gay, yet even she could see the greater good of a family made by two men in love. In the months after the twins were born, every time I visited from Louisville, Mom would clasp her hands together and fondly, even giddily, report to me the latest news on "Randy Johnson and his two little babies." She was proud of him, and perhaps on some subconscious level, proud of him for living his life authentically.

At the coffee shop on that warm Sunday in August, I found that the years had done nothing to erase the sweet disposition of the blond-haired, freckled-face boy I once knew. When he approached me in his striped polo and khaki shorts, I remembered the well-groomed Randy of my youth and was instantly drawn to him—drawn back to our time together at Belmont Baptist Church, those summer days in vacation bible school when we drank cherry Kool-Aid that tasted bitter with the sugary store-bought cookies that were doled out to us between memorizing scripture and making paperweights from plastic flowers in baby food jars. We were never close, but Randy had always felt like family to me, and we would nod and smile at each other across the pews, perhaps knowing that we were cosmically connected and destined to come together again one day to fulfill a dream for humankind. Whatever the case, it seemed there were no years between us at the coffee shop that day. We embraced as easily as siblings, although I now had to tip-toe to hug the neck of my childhood friend, who was two years my junior and hadn't been more than an inch or two taller than me the last time I'd seen him. Randy and I had reconnected on Facebook in 2011 through a mutual friend. As a result, I knew a little about Paul and their four children, Tevin, Tyler, DeSean, and Mackenzie.

Meeting Paul for the first time, I felt an instant kinship when we shook hands. He was lean and handsome in a red and white University of Louisville jersey and matching ball cap. He had baby doll eyes and a quiet demeanor that added to his mystique. Paul and Randy had just joined two other couples as plaintiffs in a lawsuit challenging Kentucky's ban on same-sex marriage.

"We want to share our story with the world," Randy told me between sips of iced tea. "We think we have some unique experiences that others could benefit from." This was his nice way of referring to the discrimination they faced as a gay couple forced into single-parent adoptions; for joint adoptions, Kentucky law required couples to be married. Although Randy and Paul had officially tied the knot in Palm Springs when gay marriage was legalized there in 2008, Kentucky did not recognize their marriage. In fact, Kentucky voters had passed a constitutional amendment in 2004 outlawing gay marriage. And all the legal and financial hurdles resulting from discriminatory laws were only part of the story. There were also the day-to-day struggles of being gay and raising multiracial children in a traditionally conservative state.

From the first minutes of our conversation, I knew that something magical would result from our meeting. Back then, I called it mojo, juju, or good energy, and I recognized whatever was at work among the three of us as a force outside of myself, a force beyond my realm of understanding—something with a purpose much bigger and more complex than writing a book. Randy and Paul would call it Divine Providence or Divine Intervention. Today I acknowledge that force as my Higher Power, and I still don't understand how it works—why people are brought together, the giant ripples that start with a pebble, the lamp we hold out to the world that shines on something unexpected. Over the next year and a half, I would immerse myself in this family's history. I would listen to their stories, comb through their photo albums, talk to the kids. I would join them for family gatherings and grow to love their dogs, Max and Sophie.

Back home, something mysterious and wonderful would happen to me in the writing process. The words would come—sometimes in a rush, sometimes after hours of pouring over notes, but almost always the process would end with a good cry. It was much like giving birth—painful and labored and highly emotional. And after reading each completed chapter, Randy and Paul would shake their heads in wonder and shed a few tears of their own. Now that it's completed I know that writing this book with them was a redemptive process for me because, like my mother, I'd had homophobic tendencies rooted in religious beliefs until a family relative was the victim of a hate crime in downtown Louisville in the early 1990s. Around the same time, the blockbuster hit movie *Philadelphia* came out, starring Tom Hanks and Denzel Washington, about a gay man with HIV unfairly fired from his job. The film's main character dies in the end, and I'd sobbed at the movie theater in realizing my own bigotry and lack of compassion.

After my conversation with Randy and Paul that bright summer day, I had a feeling something special was about to happen, and it did. The planets aligned in our favor. A power greater than myself became my muse, and somehow, through some miracle, all the love and heartache of the universe went into the making of this book. I lived the artist's dream of creating a beautiful and meaningful work that will be cherished and remembered through the ages. I am forever humbled by the honor.

Bobbi Buchanan

Foreword

Many people grow up without a father or some kind of father figure in their lives. I was lucky enough to grow up with two amazing parents, two fathers who gave me the world. I count my blessings when reflecting on what my life might have been like if it weren't for my dads. People sometimes ask me what it's like not having a mother in my life. The truth is, I don't know. I have never known life without my parents. I don't know what my life would be like if I had a mother, but I am perfectly content with that. What I know is this: you don't have to have heterosexual parents to raise you to be a decent human being.

My brothers, sister, and I had a pretty simple upbringing, or at least my parents made it seem that way. I was never treated differently in school; I was never bullied outside of school. People were nice, and it was rare if anything went less than smoothly. Little did I know, my parents spent countless hours interviewing schools, pediatricians, dentists, and virtually anyone who came into contact with us, to make sure they would not treat our family differently because they were a gay couple. It sounds excessive, but in reality, it was an intelligent thing to do because people were not automatically accepting of a young, gay, white couple raising two African-American twins.

I vividly remember going to Frankfort, Kentucky, in 2004 for a rally with my dad, Paul. The Kentucky legislature was considering putting a same-sex marriage ban on the ballot. This was a big day for my family because it put into perspective for my dads how hateful our world really was. People who didn't know us, who didn't know our family, wanted to vote on a law that would keep us from being a family and ultimately keep my parents from uniting.

I hated going to rallies solely for the reason that people were vicious. Signs that read "One Man. One Woman. God's Plan for Marriage" were plastered around the state capital that day. The halls were filled with angry people shouting mean and vile words at my dad. At nine years old, I was scarred by the sight of total strangers getting in my dad's face and yelling at him. I had no idea that the world could be that cruel. People said things like, "I'll pray for your kids" and "Your perversion is hurting your family." I will never forget how helpless I felt. After a long day enduring the hate, we started on our drive home to Louisville. "It's a sad day in Kentucky," my dad said as his voice quaked.

The memory of that day haunted me for the rest of my childhood and into my adulthood. In fact, I carried those feelings of sorrow and helplessness with me all the way to the Supreme Court on June 26, 2015. The American Civil Liberties Union offered to fly me from Louisville, Kentucky, to Washington, D.C., to hear the justices' decision on the case that my dads helped advance to the nation's highest court. I had been working with the ACLU to run my blog, "My Two Dads," to bring awareness to the same-sex marriage issue. The Supreme Court's decision would come sooner than expected. My parents had taken a vacation to New Orleans and wouldn't make it back in time to fly to the Capitol, and my brother and sister were content staying at home. The ACLU contacted me and within hours I was booked on a flight to D.C. I got off my shift from Starbucks and as I raced out the door I heard several coworkers shout, "Good luck!" and "Tell me about it when you get back." I hopped in my car and sped to the airport.

The year before, I had moved back home from college. I was transferring schools and decided that I wanted to live at home with my family while attending the University of Louisville. As my parents watched me unpack my things, they told me about our family friends Greg Bourke and Michael DeLeon, who had filed a lawsuit against the state of Kentucky and Governor Beshear to recognize their marriage, which had taken place in Canada several years prior. My dads, who were married in 2008 in Palm Springs, California, were considering joining their lawsuit to strengthen the case against the state. Shrugging it off as most eighteen year olds would, I left them with, "Cool, let me know how that goes" and went back to unpacking my room, never expecting the legal action would result in a huge victory at the national level.

Pulling up to the airport, I was excited but also nervous. The ACLU media team would meet me when I landed in D.C. that night. I went through security and walked to my terminal only to find that my flight was on a two-hour delay. I panicked. I did what anyone would do and made calls to try to get on another flight, any flight at this point.

Unfortunately, my options were limited. I had two choices: stay at home and miss what could be a historic and life-changing decision, or get on the delayed flight and be stranded in Chicago for the night. I decided on the latter. It was a huge risk, but I could not live with myself if I missed the biggest day of my family's life. We had worked so hard to get here and my parents had worked even harder for the last twenty-four years to show everyone that a same-sex couple can raise a healthy family. I wasn't going to give up that easily, especially now.

I flew into Chicago that night feeling a little defeated, though still determined. I somehow found a way to get a cab and a hotel room for the night. I set my alarm and tried to fall asleep, but my anxiety mixed with my fear of missing the alarm kept me up for a while. Four hours later, I was dressed and headed back to the airport. I skipped the coffee/breakfast combo and got through security and onto the plane. The next hour was filled with uncertainty as to where to go and whether I would even arrive in time to hear the decision.

I got off the plane and climbed into the first cab I was directed to. I was on my way to the Supreme Court. A thousand thoughts flew through my mind. I felt like I was going to Oz to ask the Wizard for something, but the Wizard was nine people, and that something was a huge request. I was basically a functioning wreck. I couldn't imagine that the justices would rule against marriage equality and my family, but if they did, I wouldn't know how to react.

When the cab finally pulled up to the Supreme Court Building, I was trembling inside. Hundreds of people with rainbow flags and signs filled the block. I made my way out of the cab, bags in tow, and found the ACLU media team. Someone on the team handed me an egg and cheese sandwich and a coffee from Starbucks. For the next hour, I had microphones in my face, talking to supporters and giving statements. I felt like a celebrity at a movie premiere and I was living for it! I gave a few quick interviews and took some pictures as ten o'clock rolled around—decision time.

Everyone looked anxious. I could see tears streaming down faces, even before anything was announced. SCOTUS blogs were pulled up on phones, and people kept refreshing their Twitter feeds, myself included. Then suddenly the interns rushed out of the Supreme Court Building and everyone fell silent. To say I was scared would be an understatement. I was petrified. What if this all fell through? What would happen if we failed? How could I face that decision? While all of these questions were racing through my mind, someone in the crowd screamed, "IT PASSED!"

Collectively, the whole block started screaming, crying, and squealing. Couples were embracing, friends were crying, people were cheering and throwing their flags in the air. Many of the traditionalists in the corner were also crying, but for different reasons. I grabbed Diana, my media strategist from the ACLU, and gave her a big hug, then texted the news to my parents. They had played a major role in this historic decision. The entire block was chanting, "Love has won!"

I waited for the plaintiffs to come out of the courtroom, and as they did, chaos ensued. I was lumped in the circle of lawyers and plaintiffs swarmed by CNN, Fox News, and other media. Amid the sea of cameras, lead plaintiff Jim Obergefell and civil rights attorney Mary Bonauto gave statements. It was havoc, but worth every moment. I spent the rest of the day doing interviews and celebrating with strangers on the streets of D.C.

We are taught from childhood through fairytales that love always wins, and believe me, it does. It was a momentous occasion for my family, and while I was sad that my parents weren't there in person, they were there in spirit. I was proud to represent the Johnson-Campion family that day. It was an unforgettable experience. Looking back nearly eleven years on what my life had been like as a nine-year-old, I remember how distraught I felt for my dads about the same-sex marriage ban in Kentucky. On June 26, 2015, however, I was elated to be in Washington, D.C., to rewrite history and redefine the American family—this time, in a way that included my family, and this time, for good.

Tevin Johnson-Campion

1: In Sickness and in Health

Randy

W hen the results of Paul's prostrate biopsy came in, I went into nurse mode. I was our family's authority on all things health-related. When the kids got sick, I doled out the medications. I monitored the fevers and checked for rashes. When someone got hurt, I checked for sprains and broken bones and assessed whether stitches would be needed. Patient care was my specialty.

So when the urologist's office called with my partner's test results, I pretended to be him. "Yes, this is Paul," I lied, rolling back from my computer and giving my full attention to the caller.

"Good afternoon, Paul. I have some news for you, if this is a good time." I recognized Dr. Stevens' gravelly voice at once. He was the gangly, gray-haired physician who had refused to acknowledge my presence during Paul's initial office visit—before the biopsies that had proven to be excruciatingly painful for Paul, procedures that I had worried about, had obsessed over, that I had wanted to know more about—details that any spouse would want to know about a loved one's care. Except in our case, I was not considered Paul's spouse. Our California marriage license was not recognized in Kentucky. Therefore, Dr. Stevens could legally ignore me, snub me, act as if I didn't exist. Because to him I obviously did not exist, and I was not an equal, and I certainly did not deserve his attention in the cold sterility of the examination room that day six months earlier when I had intended to be a buffer and a medical interpreter of sorts for Paul, my partner of twenty years. Even if I had been able to convey to Dr. Stevens my profound sense of love for Paul, the anxiety I had felt for him in that moment, and for us and our children, it wouldn't have mattered. Stevens was one of those regimented types of people who saw our love as twisted and rebellious, as though we were conspiring to turn the world on its head and undermine every facet of civilized society.

It was infuriating not only because we loved each other as any other couple—had said our vows in a marriage ritual before witnesses and the four beautiful children we had raised together—but also because I was the family's medical guru, in the same way Paul, a teacher turned counselor, was the education expert. For twenty years, we had been partners that way, pooling our knowledge and experience to manage different aspects of our household. Paul handled concerns at school, while I used my nursing expertise to take care of medical issues. We were a team.

After that day at Dr. Stevens' office, we decided to fight back. When Paul filled out the paperwork, he had listed my phone number under his contact information.

When the call came, I did not attempt to mask my voice, but I made my best effort to sound friendly the way Paul would have, despite the anger I still felt toward Stevens. "You have the results of my biopsy?"

"Yes, I do," he said. "And I'm afraid it's not all good."

I imagined Stevens hunched over his desk in his white coat with a smug grin on his face. I thought he must be joking, that he had somehow tampered with the lab report or the tissue samples. I shook my head in disbelief. "No," I said, all the technical questions I had prepared to ask slipping away from me, sliding from my consciousness into that dark, silent abyss where I'd been forced to hide my voice, my emotions, and my love for so many years.

Stevens sighed quietly. "Yes, there is a malignancy. Of the fifteen samples, fourteen turned up normal, and one showed a small number of cancer cells."

My breath escaped me as though I'd been punched in the gut. I couldn't say anything. I turned away from my office door so that no one would see the tears trickling down my cheeks. How could this be? I wondered. It must be a mistake. I wanted to blame Dr. Stevens. I didn't trust him.

"It's not a major concern. I anticipate no intervention will be necessary. We'll simply just watch and wait—that is, monitor the situation, follow up for the next ten to fifteen years."

"What?" I couldn't restrain my disbelief. Had he really just said "cancer" and "no intervention"?

He rambled on for a few minutes about the "do nothing" approach, which would mean more biopsies and more misery for Paul just to see whether the cancer grew. I jotted notes on a yellow legal pad feeling highly skeptical not only of the diagnosis, but of Stevens proposed approach for not treating it.

'If future biopsies show that there's no growth, no sign of the cancer spreading, then—"

"Could I get a copy of the slides and the lab report?" I interrupted.

There was a pause. I could hear Stevens speaking with someone in the background. "I believe we can get you those. We'll need to schedule a follow-up appointment. You'll have to sign some paperwork."

We scheduled a time, and I curtly thanked him before hanging up. I sat at my desk with my head in my hands, worrying about how I would break this news to Paul. We had both been certain there was no cancer, even after the first biopsy showed suspicious lesions. Paul had always been health conscious. He exercised regularly and watched what he ate. At forty-six years old, he was remarkably strong and lean.

It was a gray, bitterly cold February day. The ride home from work was the longest fifteen-mile journey I've ever made. Cars crawled along the freeway, darting back and forth between lanes, occasionally accelerating for short spurts, reminding me of a heart patient's dysrhythmia. Every traffic light felt like an eternity, the red glow burning like a tender wound. I wanted to get home, yet I dreaded it. Each stop sign seemed like the entrance to a time warp. I couldn't remember where I had been, or which way I was heading. It was nearly dusk by the time I got home, a hint of winter sun glowing pale orange in the western sky. Paul's Ford Explorer was already in the garage. When I walked in the house, Mackenzie looked up from her homework. "Hi, Dad!"

I kissed the top of her head and glanced at the books and papers sprawled across the kitchen table. "Everything going okay here?"

"Uh-hum," she nodded, handing me a stack of graded papers.

I thanked her and flipped through a few. "These look awesome," I said.

Mackenzie batted her dark eyes and turned a toothy grin at me.

"Where's your other dad?" She jerked a thumb in the direction of the bedroom.

I headed for the bedroom. "What about your brothers?"

She pointed at the ceiling, and I understood they were upstairs.

I drummed my thumbs as though holding an invisible game controller. "Doing this?"

She shrugged and rolled her eyes.

I called up the stairs. "Homework first! Games second!"

Their voices bounced back like an echo.

"We know!"

"We're on it!"

I winked at Mackenzie and ducked into the bedroom, closing the door behind me. I stood by the bed, wringing my hands, until Paul emerged from the bathroom. He had already changed out of his work clothes, and even in sweats, he was the picture of health with bright eyes and clear skin, like a figure straight out of a fitness magazine. I had never been the athletic type; although broad-shouldered, my features were soft, and my waist had thickened slightly over the years, while Paul had maintained the physique of an athlete. I gazed at him with adoration and a forced smile.

He stopped in his tracks. "What's wrong?"

I kept looking at him. "I got a call from the urologist today about your biopsy."

Paul gave me a pleading look.

"There's some malignancy."

The color seemed to drain from his face. Suddenly he was frail and ghost-like, this man who only seconds ago had seemed so vibrant, so durable. He stared blankly at a space between us, and when the tears welled up in his eyes, I took him in my arms and held him close and said nothing, just embraced him with my whole heart and felt the warm drops of his tears on my shoulder, wishing hard for a way to take away his fear and trembling. I would have held him forever, would have taken the cancer into my own body if I could have to spare him the hurt and the worry.

Although my mind was reeling with the possibilities, I tried to comfort him. "Everything's going to be fine, you know."

When he pulled back, he took a deep breath and closed his eyes. "I just—I need to think," he said, and he sat down on the bed to put on his tennis shoes.

I sat down next to him. "Paul, don't forget, this is the most treatable type of cancer."

I could see that he was blinking back tears. I could not remember ever seeing him this vulnerable, this afraid.

"I'm going downstairs," he said, and he stood up.

I got up and hugged him again. "We'll get through this. I promise you." I kissed his neck and let him go.

I hated for him to be alone, but I knew that he needed his space and that running on the treadmill was an outlet for him, a means of sweating out the toxins, and, I supposed, the bad feelings and negativity.

While Paul was running, I checked on the kids and then holed up in my home office, where framed copies of our marriage certificate and the vows we had taken July 3, 2008, hung on the wall across from my desk. I ran a finger over the glass, re-reading for the hundredth time the words that took me back to that sunny day in Palm Springs.

***

It was an informal wedding that we ended up including spur-of-the-moment as part of our family vacation. Several months earlier, we had booked our flight and bought airline tickets, intending to visit Paul's brother Mike and his partner for a week in early July. Coincidentally, California legalized gay marriage in June. When Mike called to invite us to get married along with him and Jim, we hastily agreed. Mike booked appointments for us to apply for our marriage licenses and made arrangements for a joint ceremony, which took place at Palm Springs City Hall, a historic brick building on a grassy oasis surrounded by palm trees.

We arrived dressed casually in clothes appropriate for 110-degree weather—the men in the family, including our thirteen-year-old twins Tevin and Tyler, and DeSean, who was nine years old, in shorts and polos. Mackenzie, our five-year-old daughter, was perhaps the most excited of our crew and the best dressed in a sundress and sandals. It was her first wedding, and she posed with everyone for photos, eager to claim her status as the lone princess of the family. Together we marched inside the building to the clerk's office, where we checked in and sat in a waiting area along with a number of other happy couples, including two men in white suits.

When our names were called, we signed a document, the clerk stamped the certificate, and we headed to the mayor's office, where one of Palm Springs' city councilmembers conducted the ceremony. Rick Hutcheson was a clean-cut man with a broad smile and a firm handshake. He welcomed us to Palm Springs and got us all situated. The children sat behind us on a leather couch with big grins on their faces. Paul and I served as witnesses for Mike and Jim, and when it was our turn, they returned the favor. We also took photos for each other.

Paul and I had exchanged rings almost sixteen years earlier. In our hearts and minds, we had been married since Christmas Day, 1992. We had made a commitment to ourselves and to the dream we shared of becoming parents and building a family of our own. But that fact did little to quell our emotions. As we stood before Councilmember Hutcheson in that cozy but business-like space, our children glowing with pride, a sense of joy came over us, and we wept quietly reciting our vows. We had declared our love and lived our lives privately, for many years in secret, to avoid controversy and backlash. I had not expected to feel so liberated and relieved by that simple little ceremony in the mayor's office and a piece of paper making everything official.

After saying "I do" and being pronounced husbands, we wiped away each other's tears and kissed for the first time in public. This was the part I had wished for, but hadn't fully imagined—to connect in this most intimate way without fear of repercussions, to meet his lips and breathe him in and become one force before God and the world. My heart was beating out of my chest, and I held onto Paul's shoulders, as much with the intention to steady myself as to embrace him. I could feel him shaking. I closed my eyes and did what came naturally. Behind us, the kids leapt to their feet, clapping and cheering.

***

From my office, I called my sisters to let them know about Paul's diagnosis. Violet and Myrtle had been my family support system over the years, accepting early on my and Paul's relationship, and rallying to our side whenever we came up against criticism or had issues to tackle. I talked first to Violet, my words rushing out like water from a flooded dam. And then I cried—this time not for Paul, but for myself, and for the very real possibility of losing him. And Violet cried with me, assuring me she would pray for healing, and that God was good, and that our love was good, and that our family was special and this would not be the end. I was exhausted and grateful by the time I hung up. Then I repeated the whole process with my sister Myrtle.

Afterward I changed clothes and washed my face, and when Paul came back upstairs, we talked for a long while about treatment options and his prognosis and what needed to be done. I would get the slides and biopsy results, and we would seek a second opinion. Neither of us was keen on Stevens. I remembered a former coworker whose husband was an urologist. I had known him years earlier, when he was a resident at University of Louisville Hospital. Our children had played together.

"I'll call him up," I told Paul, who seemed a bit lighter now, more hopeful.

That evening, we decided to break the news to the kids. We gathered the four of them at the kitchen table and explained the situation in the plainest language possible. I did most of the talking, thinking Paul might not hold up so well under the circumstances.

Mackenzie, who at nine years old was the youngest, burst into tears. I reached across the table and grabbed her hands in mine. "It's okay, honey. Dad's going to be all right. Really, he is."

Paul shifted his chair and opened his arms to her. Mackenzie slid into his embrace, her braided head pressed against his chest. Paul rubbed her back, glancing up at me. The sight of him so stricken and despondent made me feel weak, but I knew I had to be strong for him.

I got up and reached wide to hug them both, patting Mackenzie's back with one hand, squeezing Paul's shoulder with the other. I looked across the table at the boys, who seemed stunned into silence. "I know it's scary for you all to hear the word cancer." I glanced at Paul, "It's scary for us, too," I admitted, shrugging as I said it.

Paul nodded and made eye contact with each of the boys, and I knew what he was thinking, that he had to be an example for them, that he had to show them courage.

I noticed DeSean fidgeting. He was the middle child who had come to us from foster care. Paul had been his counselor in first grade. He was a sweet, easygoing young man, but seemed fraught with emotion. His fists were clenched, his lips pressed tightly together. He looked as though he wanted to run from the room. Finally, he pushed away from the table and made his way to Paul with downcast eyes, leaned over and hugged his neck. "Love you, Dad," he whispered.

Paul untangled himself from Mackenzie's embrace to hug him back. "Love you too, son," he said, his voice cracking. He reached up and tousled DeSean's short, thick curls.

The oldest boys, Tevin and Tyler, who were seventeen, maintained their composure, and as calmly and smoothly as Paul himself might have, they got up from the table to hug their father. It was a sad yet somehow beautiful moment. I was amazed at their grace, their maturity, their show of affection, and I could see how proud Paul was of them, could see how their dignity gave him strength.

How far we had come, I realized then, from that hot summer morning nearly seventeen years earlier when Paul officially adopted the twins at the courthouse in the small rural community where I had grown up thirty miles south of downtown Louisville. It was a beautiful place to live, with some of the loveliest people you'll ever meet. But it was one of the most socially backward places I've ever known—a place where a preacher could routinely use the word "nigger" without raising eyebrows, where a few families even took pride in their reputation for bullying, where anyone different was viewed with suspicion. Paul and I had started out there, in Bullitt County, moving in with my mother under the pretense of being college buddies. A few months later, we came out to her. And a few years after that, we adopted twin African-American babies.

Bullitt County was not the sort of place you came back to after going away to college, plunging headlong into cultural diversity, and discovering a whole new set of rules and logic for viewing the world. It was not the kind of community you returned to unless you returned on a mission to change it. Neither Paul nor I had believed that was part of our calling. But as I sat at our kitchen table that night thinking back on our family's unconventional beginnings, I thought maybe we had changed things. Maybe Paul and I were making the world a better place all along without even knowing it—for the sake of our love.

2: Running for My Life

Paul

Malignancy. I'd heard that word all my life, had hated the evil shape of it on my tongue when the fate of loved ones was announced, had despised its sound in my ears, the heavy thud of each syllable, the cold, dead weight of it like dirt flung from a shovel. Malignancy. Never had I expected that word to be used in a diagnosis for me, not even when Randy told me he'd gotten the call from the urologist, and his face fell, and I knew what he was about to say. And when he said it, I heard. I heard everything. It just didn't seem real, didn't seem possible.

I couldn't look at Randy. I had to steel myself against the panic, the bolts that flashed inside me, the fluttering doubt. I stared behind him at a framed photograph on our bedroom wall of Tevin and Tyler as toddlers in white shirts and bowties. The idea that I might not live to see their next birthday hit me all at once, like the gust of their twinned breath blowing out the candles. And another light flickered on the periphery of my consciousness, a daughter still so young and fragile, and from the shadows another son, one who had already known enough of the darkness of this world.

***

Randy and I had been together for three-and-a-half years when Tevin and Tyler were born. I remembered that day. Everything happened so fast. They were premature fraternal twins, arriving in the middle of the night at Lourdes Hospital in Paducah, Kentucky. The biological mother had selected us from a pool of potential adopters. That same day, February 23, 1995, we got the call from the agency: Would we be interested in twins? We never flinched. Our dream was about to come true, twice over.

We packed in a hurry and made the three-hour drive from Louisville to Paducah. When we got there, a hospital staff member showed us to the on-call suite where we would spend the next couple days caring for the babies until their weight and appetite reached acceptable levels, and they were released to go home with us.

As we waited for the nurse to bring in the boys, I paced the suite, which was set up like a studio apartment, while Randy unpacked our clothes and toiletries. Finally, the nurse wheeled in the bassinettes with our tiny bundles of love inside. Gazing at the babies, I instantly burst into tears. At four-and-a-half pounds each, they were so small and fragile that I was a little nervous about handling them at first, but Randy was confident and took the lead. He had done his clinical rotation in newborn nursing a few years earlier. I watched how he lifted one of the babies from the bassinette, and I followed suit. Once we had them in our arms and held them close to our heart, we never wanted to put them down. We would hold the boys this way, always close to our hearts, loving them unconditionally, determined to give them the best life possible.

The nurse showed us how to feed them using special nipples for smaller babies and premixed formula in bottles the size of a roll of quarters. Together we figured out how to change their diapers, and when they were wet or soiled, we reported that to the nurse on duty. We fed them every three hours, and we never asked for help. We were tired and happy and ran on pure adrenaline for the next seventy-two hours.

The whole time we were aware of the twenty-three year-old birth mother recovering in a room down the hallway. She didn't want to meet us; she didn't want to meet the babies. We could not imagine what she must have been going through. We prayed for her healing, body and soul.

I had been the one to officially adopt the twins. We had known all along, through the adoption agency, that only one of us would be permitted to become the legal guardian on paper because we were a same-sex couple.

*

It was a balmy June morning in 1995. Randy's sister Violet had agreed to accompany me in the courtroom to help with the twins. We were living with Randy's mother and stepfather at the time in a largely white, conservative area in Bullitt County, where most people knew each other—or at least knew each other's business. As a couple, we had no protection from discrimination. If the judge hearing the case was anti-gay, he could refuse to sign the paperwork with no repercussions.

Since Randy was more readily known in the community, our attorney recommended that I be the one to appear in court. She thought it would give us a more trustworthy appearance.

In the gravel parking lot outside the courthouse annex, the attorney explained what to expect.

"Let me handle everything," she said. "Only answer questions that the judge asks you directly." She turned to Randy. "You stay out here. We'll come back out as soon as the papers are signed."

Together, Randy and I hoisted the boys from the air-conditioned car in their infant carriers. Randy handed one of the carriers to Violet and hugged her gently as she gripped the handle. I could tell that he wanted to hug me, but instead he winked and gave my arm a light squeeze.

I smiled at him. "See you soon."

We turned to go inside. I felt terrible leaving him in the heat, and I hoped against hope that everything would go quickly. Despite the cool interior of the building, I never stopped sweating, and once inside the courtroom, I felt sick from nervousness. The attorney directed us to some seats near the front. The babies dozed in their carriers. They were almost four months old by then, and we had timed their mid-morning feeding so that they would be full and sleepy during the hearing.

Still, I was anxious. What if they woke up and started screaming? I imagined the judge, a man in dark-rimmed glasses with short, black hair and a distinctive voice, banging his gavel and having me and the babies removed from the courtroom without hearing our case. I imagined Judge Taylor, as the nameplate on the bench indicated, gaping at the order and firing a barrage of questions at me about my ability to care for twin babies by myself. And, naturally, I could see myself slipping up under such circumstances and saying something about my partner Randy, who was at this moment waiting in the parking lot to whisk our lovely interracial gay family back to the uncomfortable and highly precarious confines of our redneck neighborhood.

It seemed we sat there forever, and when I wasn't fretting about Judge Taylor's potential questions, I was worrying that the birth mother would suddenly appear and decide she had changed her mind about parental termination. It had happened to us before. In our first failed attempt to adopt, Randy and I had rushed to a hospital in Frankfort to meet the baby only to be waylaid by the adoption agency's counselor. "There are some signs that the mother and child are bonding," she had told us. And sure enough, the birth mother ended up reneging. A young Caucasian, she had been expecting a biracial baby, and when the infant emerged light-skinned, the barriers to raising him herself had come down.

When our case at the Bullitt County Courthouse was finally announced, we got up and stood before the bench. The judge read the order, glancing up at our attorney for answers on a few points. Within two minutes, he was signing the paperwork. All he said to me was, "Congratulations, Mr. Campion. Good luck to you and Tevin and Tyler."

I thanked him, and we exited the courtroom and caught an elevator to ground level. Randy met us just outside the door. He must have seen the excitement on my face. He broke into a huge grin, and grabbed me and pulled me into his arms before I could say a word. We lifted the babies from their carriers and covered them with kisses, and laughed and cried right there in the parking lot, not caring now whether anyone saw us, knowing only the love and the joy and the relief that we felt—and the victory. The miracle of our success. We had a family of our own now. We were a family.

***

I'm not sure how long I stood there in the bedroom waiting for reality to hit me. Perhaps I denied the cancer even while Randy took me in his arms and we sobbed together, even while my mind raced with thoughts of death, and how quickly my time on earth had gone, and how awful to have been shortchanged like this, just when the two of us had built a beautiful life for ourselves.

"I just—I need to think," I told Randy, and I got my shoes on, and I hugged him again briefly, breaking away before I could succumb to the sadness again. I needed to run—not to escape the situation, but to process what was happening to me. To accept it. To get to whatever step was next. The movement would help clear my thinking. The motion would fuel my momentum for the battle ahead.

I was used to this by now. Randy and I both were. By then we had been quietly fighting for two decades for our love and our family—to adopt children, to be recognized as parents, to be treated as equals in the eyes of society. It seemed we were always fighting battles.

I descended the steps to the basement and headed straight for the weight room, where I was surrounded by sports memorabilia from my middle and high school years—photographs and news clippings that tracked my basketball and football career achievements. I got on the treadmill, punched in the settings on the control board, and eased into a jog. I focused on breathing until I built up some speed. I checked my heart rate. My eyes kept returning to the photos lining the wall. Any other day I wouldn't have given them a second look, but this evening they called out to me like a play-by-play announcer at a tournament championship game.

How could my body have deceived me this way? I wondered. How was it deceiving me still? Maybe I was no longer a record-breaking athlete, but I still felt good physically, felt as good as I ever had. Having cancer seemed surreal.

Perhaps I was still in denial. Maybe I was thinking on some subconscious level that denying the cancer would keep it from killing me. And yet I couldn't stop thinking of dying—whether it would be slow and excruciating, or quick and efficient in taking me down; whether I had time to write up a living will, and whether it would even be respected.

I glimpsed down at the control panel, saw that I was hitting the two-mile mark, and braced for the incline and the familiar ache of fatigued thighs. My goal was six miles, which was more than my usual daily regimen, but physical feats had never been too difficult for me. I hadn't run six miles in months, yet I had every confidence I could complete the course, even if I doubted my ability to beat the cancer. Physical hurdles were a cinch. Medical obstacles were more of a challenge. But what plagued me most at that moment were the legal difficulties of my dying. I worried what it would mean for Randy and the boys. We had known for seventeen years that there would be snags for us. With each adoption—first Tevin and Tyler, then Mackenzie, whom Randy adopted, then DeSean—we learned more about the complications in interpreting laws when the situation involved gay couples. In short, I knew that if anything happened to me, my father, who had remained distant after I came out to him and my mother, would have had more say-so over the boys than Randy—that legally, my father (and my mother, if she hadn't died in 2006) would have been considered next of kin.

The endorphins kicked in at three miles, flooding my shattered nerves. I had finished a mile in eight minutes.

***

In October 1995, four months after the adoption became official, Randy and I made our first road trip with the twins to visit my family in Jamestown, New York. I had been estranged from my parents since coming out to them in 1988, but had managed a truce, at least temporarily. At thirty years old, I was hoping for acceptance, but more importantly, I wanted my mother and father to have a relationship with the boys—their grandsons. Randy felt strongly about the matter, too, and had even volunteered to stay at the hotel once we got there to avoid any tension between my parents and us.

With the boys being only eight months old, we planned the 500-mile trip so that we could stop about halfway, grab a motel room, and rest for a few hours. Our stop landed us in Medina, Ohio, a small, seemingly quiet town off Interstate 71 about thirty miles south of Cleveland. After checking in, while we were carrying the twins across the parking lot to the room, I noticed a young lady in the lobby glaring at us.

"Look at that." I nudged Randy.

He shot her a cold look over his shoulder. "Pfft. What are you staring at?"

The lady in the lobby was nothing new to us. We had grown used to people's reactions when they saw us in public with the boys, two young white men with two tiny black babies. It was often a mix of surprise and curiosity, but frequently there was suspicion, and sometimes even hostility—particularly when Randy and I were together, and the onlookers caught on to the fact that we were a gay couple.

Inside the room, we forgot about the incident and started getting ready for bed. We changed the boys' diapers and tucked them into bed between us, where they promptly fell asleep. I had just turned off the lights and slipped back into bed when we were startled by pounding on the motel room door.

"Police! Open up!"

The boys began bawling, and I tended to them while Randy answered the door.

Two Medina police officers flashed their badges and shined a flashlight into the darkened room.

"What seems to be the problem?" I demanded, holding Tyler against me while I turned on a lamp. Randy picked up Tevin and scrambled around searching for a pacifier or baby bottle.

The officers were large men, and they entered the room slowly, scanning the premises as though expecting booby traps. The taller one addressed us while his partner peeked in the bathroom. "We got a report of suspicious activity."

Tyler's face crumpled at the sound of the officer's voice and his cries grew louder. I stroked his back and rocked him gently. "The only suspicious thing going on here is the police creating a ruckus and waking up two babies in the middle of the night."

The taller officer straightened his back, his face contorted. "Sir, we are here for their safety, and I would advise you to refrain from insults like that or I'll have to arrest you for disorderly conduct."

I glared at him but said nothing.

Randy had managed to calm Tevin down, and he came around to my side of the bed with the baby on his hip. "We're just trying to get a little sleep," he reasoned.

"Where are you headed with these little ones?" the officer asked.

I didn't think it was necessary to answer, but Randy obliged. "We're headed to Jamestown, New York—"

"What does it matter where we're going? We haven't committed a crime," I interrupted.

The taller officer held out a hand while his partner stepped forward, folding his arms across his chest. They both eyed me as though I were a disobedient child. Suddenly, I was reminded of what I had in store when we got to New York.

"Now, look," the officer said, his voice gruff. "There's no need to get nasty. We are here to do our job. We were called to come here out of concern for these children. If you care at all about them, then you will cooperate."

I didn't appreciate his condescending tone but remained silent.

"Okay," Randy replied. "What else do you need to know? We're going to visit family."

The officer pulled a small notebook from his pocket and took down our names and address. His partner called in our driver's licenses' information over his portable radio for a background check.

"Is that your white Nissan Pathfinder in the parking lot?"

"Yes," I said.

"And whose children are these?"

I stood up. "They're ours."

"Sir, please stay seated."

I sat on the bed. "We adopted them from birth. We've had them all eight months of their lives."

The officers looked at each other with raised eyebrows.

"Do you have some sort of proof—adoption papers? Birth certificates? Social security cards?"

I blew out an exasperated sigh. "That's just not something you pack on a family trip. I mean, how many parents do you know that routinely carry that stuff around?"

The officer shrugged. "In your case, you need to do that. You are obviously not their biological parents." He paused, shifting his feet. "And you two are related?"

"We're a couple," I interjected before Randy had time to respond. "Yes, we're gay, and yes, we are the fathers of two African-American children."

The taller officer's mouth twitched. His partner stepped back and rolled his head as though stretching a cramped neck.

Tevin and Tyler had stopped crying but were restless now. Tyler was hugging my neck, his sleepy head bobbing on my shoulder. Tevin had cupped Randy's face in his hands and was babbling something incoherent.

The officer smiled in spite of himself and was about to say something when the call came in over the radio reporting our background checks as clean.

"Looks like you're in the clear." His voice was softer now but still grating.

I couldn't wait for them to leave. I walked over to open the door.

On his way out, the officer pivoted. "I would recommend you start carrying that paperwork when you travel out of state," he said.

I nodded, closed the door, and leaned against it for a minute. Randy blew out his breath. We didn't get much sleep that night. I hoped this was not an omen of how the rest of the trip would play out. I began to wonder if it had been a bad idea.

***

I ran the fourth mile in seven minutes. My legs no longer seemed a part of me; they were running of their own accord. But I knew if I allowed myself to think about my body's motion too deeply, I would collapse with exhaustion. I pondered the wall of old photographs and recalled how proud my parents had been in those days. I remembered how cold my father had turned when I told him and Mom that I was gay, remembered the shame and disappointment in my mother's eyes. I wondered how they could have denied me their love that way, knowing now the unconditional love I felt for my own children. I had to doubt that they themselves had ever experienced the depth of that love.

***

I hadn't seen my parents in seven years when I took the twins to visit for the first time, the same trip that seemed destined for failure after the run-in with the Medina police. After helping me pack the diaper bags and strap the boys into their car seats, Randy stood in the parking lot of the Jamestown Red Roof Inn and watched us leave. I eyed him in the rearview mirror, still smiling and waving at us. A twinge of anger rose up inside me over having to leave the love of my life this way, once again, in a parking lot. And for what? I wondered. The comfort of others? Or was it the discomfort that others felt over matters of the heart?

My resentment soon gave way to nervousness and then to melancholy. For most of the short drive, I kept checking the twins in the rearview mirror. Seeing them made my heart melt. I couldn't imagine ever rejecting them, no matter what happened. I fretted over how my mother and father might respond to them.

It was a cool October morning, and, in the historic parts of Jamestown, older hardwood trees were aglow with fall foliage. When I pulled into the driveway, I felt slightly disoriented. The house seemed smaller. Everything seemed different somehow. There was no one there to greet me, so I unloaded the boys by myself, threw a diaper bag over each shoulder, and lugged both baby carriers single-handedly across the yard to the back door.

My father appeared first, and I was shocked to see how much he had aged, how the creases in his skin had deepened, how his hair had thinned to a silver mist. When I got inside and set the carriers down, he hugged me, and I was surprised not only by the sudden show of affection, but also because it was the first time my father had ever embraced me. I went from Dad's arms directly to Mom's. She was crying, and she held me much longer than she ever had, smelling of roses and Aqua Net.

Mom ushered us into the living room, and I got the boys from their carriers and took their coats off. Tyler cried when I handed him off to Dad, so I took him back and held both babies on my lap for a while, until they got comfortable with their surroundings.

"So they sleep through the night now?" Dad asked.

"Oh, yes. They've been pretty good about that for the past couple months."

"Now, which one's Tevin and which is Tyler?" Mom wanted to know. "And how do you tell them apart?"

I laughed. "Well, for one thing, Tyler's a little bit smaller."

Mom spread a blanket on the floor and urged me to let them down. I pulled some toys from the diaper bags and sat them down. Mom watched them with smiling eyes. She marveled over their hair. "It's so thick!" she exclaimed.

Slowly, the boys warmed up to her and to Dad. My sister Maura came over at some point, and the three of them fawned over the babies, and took great interest in all my stories about them. But when I mentioned Randy, I noticed them steering away from the conversation, or turning the discussion in another direction. It was almost as if Randy didn't exist to them, and this visit, unfortunately, would set the tone for all future visits. My parents would never ask about Randy, would never inquire about his career or his mother and siblings. Over the course of the next several years, they would avoid every mention of "Daddy Randy" by the boys.

We stayed for a couple hours that day, and when I left to get the boys back to the hotel for a nap, I felt good about the visit and filled with hope. I had hated the long separation from my family. I wanted more than anything to have them all back in my life. But over time, that longing would prove to be an impossibly high hope. Nothing had changed. My parents would not acknowledge Randy, and my mother would "encourage" several of my siblings to treat him as an outsider. When my brother Chris invited the two of us to his wedding, my mother would protest. The friction was so intense that Randy and I would decide not to go, though we would remain close to Chris, and to my sister Kate and my brother Mike. Although they represented only half of my divided family, their support and acceptance over the years would mean the world to me. And their love would always be enough.

***

I pushed with everything I had for the final mile, the sixth mile. I had rejoined my limbs and torso, the strain of my stride wracking my body. My lungs were burning; my hamstrings were on fire. Yet when I checked the control board, I realized I would not beat my time. I would not meet my goal. Defeat weighed heavy on me. I was done, finished. I slowed my pace and started cooling down. Was it simply my time?

Something had to be done about the kids. I could not die peacefully, or even channel my energy into fighting the cancer, knowing their fate ultimately might be in the hands of my father—a man who barely knew them, who could not possibly love and care for them the way my partner did.

When the treadmill stopped, the footfalls of my children echoed on the floors above me.

3: Fair Treatment

Randy

After we broke the news to the kids about Daddy Paul's diagnosis, I called my friend Ganesh Rao, the urologist. Although we hadn't spoken in a few years, Ganesh was cordial and remembered our children playing together. He asked about the twins.

"They're doing great," I told him. "Tevin's at Trinity High School now. He wants to study journalism. Tyler's going to Manual, the performing arts school. He loves the theater—theatrical arts. They stay busy. How are your kids?"

Paul was pacing between the bedroom and the living room, eager for some answers but apparently too nervous to stand still and listen to our small talk.

We chatted about the kids for a few minutes, bemoaning their hasty growth and celebrating their accomplishments. I eased into the subject of Paul's diagnosis. "You remember my partner, Paul?"

"Sure, I do. How is he?"

"Well, the reason I'm calling is that we're having a bit of a medical crisis. Paul just had a second biopsy for prostate cancer, and the results show there's malignancy in one of the tissue samples."

"I see," replied Ganesh, without hesitation. "This must be upsetting for you both, but we have ways to treat it. This can be taken care of."

I appreciated his reassuring tone. "That's good to hear because we're looking for a second opinion."

"I would be happy to help with that," he said. "Can you get the biopsy results and bring them to our office? I would like to have our pathologist look at them to confirm the diagnosis."

"Yes, I've already requested those." I grabbed a pen and some paper from a drawer and made a note to remind myself. "The doctor who did the biopsies said he didn't think treatment was needed at this point. His recommendation is to just monitor the situation."

Ganesh grunted. "Well, that depends on the patient, to some degree. How much stress will that add to the situation? Every time Paul has an ache, will he be afraid that it's the cancer spreading? These things must be considered."

"Exactly," I chimed in, scribbling more notes and catching Paul's eye as he walked into the bedroom again. I pointed at the receiver and mouthed the words to him, "He's on this!"

Paul stopped and bowed his head, waiting, I presumed. Or maybe praying, I thought a minute later.

"There are several options in a case like this. Surgically removing the prostate, which is called a prostatectomy, is sometimes the best way to go to ensure you have removed the cancer. The risks are higher, but so are the success rates, and the long-term prognosis is much better."

I wrote down "Surgical removal" and gave Paul a thumbs-up. "What about the risks for surgery?"

"Nerve damage is perhaps the highest risk," said Ganesh. "Urinary dysfunction. Some erectile dysfunction. These are fairly common side effects in the months immediately following surgery, and even after some of the other treatment options, but they are not usually severe. Typically patients return to pre-treatment levels within the first year."

Paul paced the bedroom for another minute or two, then left the room again while Ganesh described the advantages and disadvantages of using direct radiation to eradicate the cancer.

"If we choose radiation first, then there will be no option for surgery in the future. What happens is the radiation zaps the tissue so that there's nothing left to remove. However, cancer cells can remain in the body even after the tissue has been radiated," he explained.

"There's also a method of radiation treatment that entails planting radioactive seeds in the prostrate. The risks are much lower, and in some cases, this method can be as effective as surgery."

"Uh-huh," I replied, jotting everything down so that I could explain the options to Paul later.

"How old is Paul?" Ganesh asked.

"He's forty-six," I answered.

"You know, he might be a candidate for the da Vinci prostatectomy." Ganesh's voice went up an octave.

"Da Vinci?" It sounded familiar to me as a medical procedure.

"Yes. Da Vinci, as in Leonardo, the artist who painted the Mona Lisa. It's a minimally invasive robotic procedure. Very precise and very effective. If you are interested in this, you and Paul must meet with my partner, Bradley Bell. He is one of the leading Da Vinci prostatectomy surgeons in the country."

"No way!" I wanted to reach through the phone and hug Ganesh. It couldn't have been luck. I felt certain that Divine Providence had led us to him. "That sounds great. We would love to find out more about it."

I agreed to drop off Paul's biopsy results as soon as we received them, and we set up an appointment for the following week.

"Thank you so much, Ganesh. I can't tell you how much this means to us."

"It's no problem," he said.

After I hung up, I could feel my shoulders slump in relief. I got up and went to find Paul.

***

I was not looking forward to the follow-up appointment with Dr. Stevens. I knew it would be painful and awkward not only because of Paul's diagnosis, but also because of the doctor's chilly demeanor toward us. He had been cold and uncaring throughout Paul's office visit and biopsy, making it quite clear that he disapproved of our relationship. Our sole mission in returning to his office was to sign the paperwork required to get the tissue slides and biopsy report. We had decided on the drive over that nothing he said mattered. We were not only seeking a second opinion, but we were finding a new doctor—one who didn't grit his teeth or shudder as though he might spontaneously combust if forced to spend another minute with us.

The waiting room was crowded that day, and we settled into a cramped space expecting to be there for a while, but Dr. Stevens himself leaned out the door thirty minutes later and called Paul back.

When I slipped in behind Paul, Stevens sneered at me, spun around without a word, and started down the hallway. We followed him through a plain white door that I assumed would lead into a private office. I was surprised to see it was the staff break room, sparsely furnished with a couple tables and chairs. There was a sink with a microwave on the counter and a standard-sized refrigerator. A large window overlooked the parking lot.

Dr. Stevens sat down with a clipboard and manila folder, as though he routinely met with patients in the break room. "Now, let's see…" he began. He never glanced up or asked us to join him.

While he rifled through the paperwork, Paul and I exchanged doubtful looks, gave up on waiting for an invitation, and took the two seats across from him.

As he had done during all previous visits, Stevens addressed Paul and avoided eye contact with me. At some point, I noticed that even his posture rejected me; he sat cross-legged, with his torso turned toward Paul, his forearms pressed to the table, as though shielding the medical documents that lay in front of him.

"As I mentioned on the phone, there are several options for treating the malignancy."

I leaned forward and opened my mouth to protest, but Paul nudged me with his knee. I turned to him, wide-eyed, shaking my head to let him know that no options had been discussed. Paul nodded to let me know he understood.

Stevens talked right over our antics. "The first option is prostatectomy, and that involves full surgical removal of the prostate gland. It's a common procedure. I've performed it hundreds of times myself."

Paul leaned forward, in spite of himself. "What are the risks with the surgery?" he asked. Although Ganesh had explained those, I hadn't mentioned them to Paul yet. I could sense his apprehension, his impatience, and I had to restrain myself from reaching over and giving him a quick, reassuring hug, I was sure Stevens would have rather gouged out his own eyeballs than witness such unscrupulous behavior.

"Of course, there are risks with every alternative." Stevens waved a hand. It was his typically vague response.

"What about the prognosis for recovery?" Paul asked.

Stevens slouched, glaring at Paul as though it was the silliest question a patient had ever asked. His steely blue eyes shifted about the room while he appeared to dream up an answer. "The prognosis is good as long as the cancer is confined to the prostate. But, of course, we can't determine that until the prostate gland is removed."

He cleared his throat and started digging through the stack of papers. He pulled out a document and placed it on the table in front of Paul. "You'll need to read and sign this for the biopsy results."

Paul turned the paper slightly so that I could read it, too. Stevens ignored me, although I sensed that internally he was rolling his eyes.

"Another option is to simply watch and wait to see whether the cancer spreads," he said. "Many men die with prostate cancer, but not because of it," he stressed, sliding a pen across the table.

After signing the paper, Paul pushed it back toward Stevens along with the pen. The doctor snatched them up and began packing up the rest of his documents in silence.

Paul exhaled and turned to me, the stress evident in his sullen expression. I could see that he had questions, but it was obvious that he didn't want to ask them here. I couldn't blame him. I jerked my head in the direction of the door and pushed my chair back an inch or two.

Paul took the cue and scooted back from the table. "I think we're going to need some time to research our options and get back with you."

Stevens shrugged slightly, as though insulted. Then, without speaking, he got up, slipped his pen into his pocket, and gathered his clipboard and folder. He pointed us toward the exit and parted in the opposite direction. I led Paul out, one hand on his back, the other clutching the envelope that held all the questions about our future.

***

Before our appointment with Dr. Bell, Paul and I researched options for treatment on the Internet. I could tell that Paul was still anxious about the diagnosis. The joy had gone out of him, the softness in his features replaced with a hard grimace. Stevens had said nothing to ease his mind, and neither of us had been comfortable talking with him about potential side effects such as erectile dysfunction.

I located some statistics on cure rates through the American Cancer Society's website and read the information aloud to Paul in the living room after dinner one evening. "Listen to this: 'To get fifteen-year survival rates, doctors have to look at men who were treated at least fifteen years ago. Improvements in detection and treatment since then may result in a better outlook for people now being diagnosed with prostate cancer.'"

I looked up at Paul, who sat on the couch across from me scrolling through the pros and cons of prostate surgery.

"The fifteen-year survival rate is ninety-four percent," I informed him. "That's really good, especially since we're talking about patients who were diagnosed fifteen years ago. We've made huge strides in medical technology since then," I assured him.

Paul nodded, his expression unchanged, and kept reading.

"Ganesh was very upbeat the other day," I told him. "And I don't think he was just trying to be nice."

Paul managed a tight smile and glanced around to make sure the kids weren't around. "That's great, Dad, but I'm concerned about my sex life, too."

Until then, I hadn't wanted to let on that I was concerned about that myself. Neither of us would deny the fact that sex was a factor in the equation for our happiness as a couple. Paul didn't say so, but I knew incontinence was another worry, and rightfully so. The possibility of needing to wear diapers for the rest of your life was awful to think about, particularly for someone as active as Paul had been.

My throat tightened and my eyes grew watery. I reached over to pat his leg, caressing the fabric of his blue jeans. His hand clasped mine, and a sharp, tiny jolt hit me, all his fears flowing into me like an electric current—the cancer, the children, the pain and exhaustion of hiding our love, of endless hurdles and the same old hurts from our pasts coming back again and again, the ugly fat and gristle boiling to the surface. Paul's cancer made clear our struggle. It wasn't just a matter of him surviving, but a question of our living. We would have to insist that the world move out of our way.

4: Finding the Right Doctor

Paul

After what could only be described as a harrowing experience with a homophobic urologist, Randy and I rode together to the office of another urologist—one who had offered to give a second opinion on my prostate cancer diagnosis. Dr. Bradley Bell worked in the same practice as our friend, Dr. Ganesh Rao. We hoped for a more pleasant experience with Dr. Bell—if not a different diagnosis, then at least the assurance that I would receive the best treatment, regardless of my sexual orientation.

Randy drove while I sat quietly in the passenger seat, feeling nervous and making mental notes of the questions I wanted to ask. We hit morning rush-hour traffic crossing the bridge from downtown Louisville into Jeffersonville, where the urology team's office was located. The ride was stop-and-go for twenty minutes. I worried we might be late, but Randy waved a hand dismissively. "They know this traffic gets crazy," he said. "They're not going to send us home for being a couple minutes late."

We arrived with five minutes to spare. The building was a new modern design, several stories high, with lots of glass and an attractive layout. We strode from the parking lot into the building, which was spacious and busy inside, with medical staff and patients milling about. There was a homey feel to the décor. The lighting was mostly natural, and the walls and floors were neutral tones. I noticed immediately how inviting the waiting area seemed, despite being a large, open space. A TV was mounted over a creek-stone fireplace, and there were several magazine racks and ample chairs with cushioned backs and armrests arranged in a horseshoe pattern.

After checking in, we waited only a few minutes to see Dr. Bell, a short, handsome man with perfectly coifed blond hair and a firm handshake. We met with him in a small, windowless exam room painted in warm, earthy colors. I realized then that the entire office had that same welcoming quality, which contrasted starkly with the other urologist's cold, white, antiseptic space.

"Dr. Rao has told me a lot about your case," said Dr. Bell, speaking first to me but turning immediately to include Randy in the conversation. "We've had a look at your biopsy samples, and the results reported by Dr. Stevens have been confirmed. There is cancer in one of the samples.

I could feel my body slumping and the warm weight of Randy's hand on my shoulder.

Dr. Bell frowned. "I'm sure that's not what you wanted to hear, and I don't blame you one bit, Paul." He looked at me hard, and his sincerity showed. "There are so many options for this level of treatment, and they're all very effective."

I nodded. "Dr. Rao was very thorough in explaining what's available."

"Good," Dr. Bell said, smiling.

"Could you tell us more about this da Vinci procedure?" Randy asked. "I hear it's very high tech."

"Of course." Dr. Bell pulled out a diagram to show us how it worked. "You probably know that there are risks that go along with the surgery."

"We've done some research," Randy admitted with a grin.

"Well, what's great about the da Vinci is that it allows the type of precision a surgeon needs to not only remove the cancerous prostate, but to do it in a way that spares the neurovascular bundles on either side of the prostate."

He pointed to the location of the prostate in a figure of a male torso on the diagram.

"In that way, we can preserve the patient's sexual potency and urinary continence," he added. "Of course, those are usually the topmost concerns to patients in terms of side effects."

"That's definitely been a concern of mine," I said, and I leaned in closer to have a better look at the diagrams.

Dr. Bell wagged his head. "It's really pretty cool stuff." His eyes widened. He was obviously a big believer in the technology. "The results have been phenomenal."

Randy elbow bumped me. I glanced up at him and could tell by his buoyant expression that he had a good feeling about Dr. Bell. This was

Paul

often our way in making critical, life-altering decisions. We went by vibes. We prayed. We believed in Divine Intervention.

Dr. Bell was upbeat when he asked, "Now what questions do you have for me?"

I looked at him and smiled, with every confidence that he was the right doctor. I could hear it in his voice. He seemed ready for anything.

***

We'd been through the business of finding the right doctor for the twins seventeen years earlier. The day we took Tevin and Tyler to the pediatrician for their one-week checkup, they looked like Kewpie dolls with their big brown eyes and coffee-black skin, their tiny arms and torsos swimming inside the quilted lining of puffy newborn coats. They had weighed in at about four pounds each at birth, so almost everything was baggy at first. Sleeves and pant legs had to be rolled up. Hats drooped over their faces. Booties slipped off their feet.

Their smallness made them more beautiful and precious to Randy and me, but also underscored their vulnerability, especially in a rural Southern community that seemed stuck in the last century.

There were no other black children where we lived. We did not have black neighbors, black teachers, or black business owners in Bullitt County. In the most progressive part of the county, where I taught elementary school, there were one or two black students out of the five hundred or so enrolled at any given time. My only other experience with local race relations happened soon after I moved in with Randy at his mother's house on Delk Road in 1992. It was a brown brick cape-cod style home that sat on an acre of flat ground with flowerbeds and a few massive trees. There were swings on both ends of the porch and large ferns that hung along the front. It was a big, inviting home in a seemingly all-American country setting. The only downfall, I would soon realize, was the backwardness of some of the people who lived there.

*

29

We had gone to the neighborhood convenience store for sandwich fixings. The store sat about a half-mile north on the main highway near a strip of modest homes and next door to a small church that had once been the local skating rink. We had just walked out of the store when a mud-splattered, four-by-four pickup truck rumbled into the parking lot with a Confederate flag hoisted in its bed. It was the first time I'd ever seen the flag outside a book or a movie. I felt like I had traveled back in time, and I quickly scanned the parking lot to be sure no black person was around to witness this atrocity. A young man in cowboy boots and blue jeans tumbled out of the cab and hawked a mouthful of brownish liquid onto the pavement. He wore a tank top with an American flag and bald eagle on it, and I remember thinking how ironic, to fly both flags. After he ambled into the store, I stood there staring at the flag in the bed of the pickup with my jaw hanging open, a wave of nausea washing over me. For me, the flag symbolized a hatred and intolerance of black people, powerful enough to justify murder. I'd read the horrific accounts of lynchings that occurred across the United States following the Civil War and the long, sordid histories of violence and racism perpetuated by Jim Crow laws and white supremacists who laid claim to the Confederate flag. In my mind, the flag was a warning, and the warning it screamed at me was, "No Blacks!"

That attitude had not disappeared and showed no signs of dissipating three years later, when we became parents. We knew that eventually we would have to move into the city in order for our children to grow up in a nurturing, racially tolerant environment, just as we knew we would have to seek a pediatrician in Louisville to get the boys the best health care treatment possible without prejudice. Finding a pediatrician was the easier step to accomplish, and the more urgent one when the twins were newborn babies.

It was icy cold on the morning of their one-week checkup in early March. We got up extra early to get the boys ready. We had established a routine by then. Randy sterilized bottles while I laundered spit-up blankets and baby clothes. As Randy mixed and measured formula, I bathed the babies, one at a time, and dressed them in footed rompers to stave off the chill of winter.

After their morning feeding, we bundled up the boys in their oversized outerwear and carried them from the house to the car, both of us glancing around, hopeful that the neighbors were still in bed and not watching out their windows. Although Randy's family understood we were a couple, we had not announced our relationship publicly, preferring instead to let people assume we were roommates. However, we knew that when people saw us with the babies, our secret would be out. I worried what would happen. My main concern was for the safety of the boys.

Leaving Belmont was always a relief, and when we reached the main highway, I let out a sigh. Tevin and Tyler dozed on the thirty-minute ride to the pediatrician's office I'd found through my insurance company. It was the first time we had been out since the babies were born. We had stayed cooped up with them at the house and had bonded with them in that first week. I can't remember how we'd spent our spare time before the twins arrived, but I remember well how we adjusted to the around-the-clock routine of feeding the boys and changing their diapers. We were happy and tired, exhausted and emotional. Like any couple, we'd had our spats. But with the twins, we no longer had the time or the energy to fuss at one another, much less complain about the workload or second-guess our abilities as parents. All our efforts focused on caring for these two brand new precious lives.

Pediatric & Neonatal Specialists was located in one of Louisville's southernmost suburbs, an area known as Okolona. The office was among several occupants in a sprawling, single-story medical building in the heart of the neighborhood's business district. We arrived early, and Randy signed us in. Since the babies were awake, we slipped off their coats and took them out of their carriers. Other parents in the waiting room instantly perked up.

A heavyset lady with a chubby toddler on her lap eyed us appreciatively. "They are so cute," she said. "Twins?"

Randy and I nodded and smiled back at her.

"How old are they?" a young lady with a pierced nose and heavy eye makeup wanted to know.

"Just over a week," I answered, and leaned over to peek at the baby in her arms. "How about yours?"

"Six weeks," she replied. "But she looks like a cow compared to those two!"

We laughed. "Twins tend to be smaller," Randy explained.

All eyes turned to Tevin and Tyler. Soon the waiting area was buzzing with conversation. We talked easily with an array of women—first-time mothers and experienced ones, breastfeeding moms and bottle feeders, cloth-diaper users and advocates of disposable. They wanted to know about our experiences and were quick to offer us advice. Most were polite and accepting, although a few stayed quietly in the background, casting weary glances our way.

When the receptionist asked me to fill out patient paperwork, I entered my information under "Father," then scratched out "Mother," and wrote "Father" above it, adding Randy's information. No one in the office ever questioned this. It was all we had to do in that office to be recognized equally as parents of the boys.

The mostly female office staff took great interest in our family. They crowded around and doted on the babies as they were weighed and measured. In the exam room, we answered the nurse's questions about the twins' eating and sleeping patterns. We showed her the logbook in which we had recorded the feeding times and the ounces of formula each baby had consumed. She took some time to review it. "Looks like you're doing a terrific job with these two," she concluded, handing back the notebook and informing us that the doctor would be in to see us soon.

Dr. Charles Sarasohn was a soft-spoken man with graying hair. He was gentle in examining the babies. He checked their tummies and their umbilical cords, tested their reflexes, and used a stethoscope to listen to their hearts.

"They both appear to be in excellent health," he reported while jotting some notes on a clipboard. "What questions do you have for me?" he asked, and his kind eyes met both mine and Randy's.

Randy and I exchanged smiles. My heart made a tiny leap in my chest as I gazed at my partner, who, it seemed, had never doubted this moment for an instant. I nearly cried right then and had to turn away quickly and focus on the son in my arms, whichever one he happened to be—Tevin or Tyler, it made no difference; all that mattered was this wave of love unfurling inside me like giant sails on an ocean. I wanted to clap and cheer. I wanted to shout, "Hallelujah!" Instead, I looked up at Dr. Sarasohn, closed my eyes, and made a slight bow with my head. "Thank you, doctor," I said. "Thank you for everything."

5: Divine Providence

Randy

The experiences that Paul and I had with our friend Ganesh Rao and his colleague, Dr. Bradley Bell, affirmed my faith in God. I believed in Divine Providence. I believed that God had a plan for Paul and me. Through all the hardship we had endured adopting children and raising them under the scrutiny of a world reluctant to think two gay men could properly bring up a family, I felt the presence of a higher power, and I trusted that power to see us through.

I hadn't always felt that way, though. Before meeting Paul, I had denied my sexuality and questioned my faith. I blamed those internal conflicts on my indoctrination at Belmont Baptist Church in my youth.

***

On a sweltering Sunday morning in the summer of 1980, I learned about evil from a stocky, red-faced country preacher in the little Baptist church just across the railroad tracks from where I lived. I could see the steeple from my bedroom window, and on those rare occasions when my mother and I didn't make it for the service, I could hear from my back yard the two-toned gong of the bell pealing to signal the start of worship. For years afterward, the sight of that church and the sound of that bell conjured mostly good memories for my mother and the neighborhood kids, but for me that white clapboard building at the end of Church Avenue in the tiny town of Belmont became a hurtful, hateful symbol of the intolerance and bigotry I endured as a child. And it all started with that summer sermon.

The preacher wore a light gray suit and baby blue necktie, his jacket unbuttoned, his index finger occasionally slipping into his shirt collar and sliding around his neck to loosen the damp, white fabric's hold. "Let me tell you where our nation is heading," he shouted, raising an arm and pivoting at the pulpit, his black leather shoes pointing first at the congregation on the right, then shifting to the left.

I sat fidgeting next to my mother, Frances, in our usual spot in a pew near the back, a safe distance from the condemnation the preacher spewed week after week against feminists, homosexuals, and African Americans.

"We're headed for destruction!" the preacher shrieked, and when his fist came down on the podium, I jerked and blinked from the force of it.

I was not afraid of Brother O'Dell, but I disliked him, and his sermons made me edgy. At twelve years old, I knew I was gay but worked desperately to hide my sexuality to avoid the jeers and teasing. In elementary school, other boys had made fun of the way I talked and how I looked. "You have a girl butt," they sneered. "You must like boys!" I had denied their accusations. Because of the constant bullying, I had often pretended to be sick as an excuse to stay home from school. As I grew older, I learned how to keep my secret in check. I started using the word "faggot" in casual conversations and accused others of being gay before they had a chance to accuse me.

I did everything possible to keep from being discovered, which was my greatest fear—especially at church. Especially Belmont Baptist Church. I thought the preacher knew. I worried that he would call me out and humiliate me in front of the whole church, that I would be dragged to the altar and forced to repent.

The preacher was waving his King James Bible in the air and shaking his head. "We are fighting a holy war," he cried. "Our nation is facing the greatest evil of this century right here on our soil!" He stomped on the pulpit, but the blow was muffled by its crimson carpet.

Before this, my mother and I had endured years of lengthy Pentecostal church services where those who were touched by the spirit spoke in tongues, collapsed at the altar, and twitched in the aisles in a sort of seizure. Compared to those experiences, Belmont Baptist Church and Brother O'Dell were not so frightening. While he frequently shouted and his face often flushed with anger, his voice was thin and lacked force. When he spoke, and particularly when he preached, he tended to leave off the soft consonants at the end of words. For example, "Jesus Christ" sounded more like "Jesus Cry." His grammar was often faulty, too, and that gave me some level of comfort, as though because of that fact I might be able to dismiss his words, his message, his hateful tone.

The preacher moved out from behind the podium, away from the microphone, and shook his fist at the congregation.

"If you think woman's rights is a good thing ... If you think abortion is a good thing ... if you think homosexuals deserve some kind of special rights, I'll tell ya what, brother, you're headed straight for a devil's hell," he squealed, his voice as shrill and scratchy as an old 45 RPM record.

I held my breath and glanced around nervously. The women fanned their faces with church programs while the men mopped their brows with white handkerchiefs. A few muttered "Amen!"

The preacher removed his wire-rimmed glasses and wiped the sweat from his forehead and the back of his neck. "Abortion is murder! Woman has no right to defy the law of God, handed down to Moses on Mount Sinai." He darted back to the podium, shoved his glasses back on, and flipped through the pages of his bible. His finger stabbed the page to emphasize each word as he read aloud: "Thou ... Shalt ... Not ... Kill! Right here, Exodus, chapter twenty, verse thirteen!"

A few congregation members, including one or two women, shouted their approval.

"'Well, preacher,' you say, 'that's feminism.'" He frowned and wagged his head. "You call it feminism, I call it evil!"

More shouts of "Amen!" followed.

"And I'll tell you something else." His eyes slowly scanned our faces, from the front to the back rows. It felt as though they came to rest on me. I stared back, trying not to blink. "I'll tell you straight from the word of God. It's in Genesis." He raised an eyebrow at me, nodded once, then pointed to the bible spread open on the podium. I quickly retrieved mine from the pew and waited for further instruction. Everyone bowed over their bibles, skimming Genesis for the reference.

"In Sodom and Gomorrah, they was destroyed for their wickedness. That's what America is coming to if we don't stop this perversion of homosexuality. You say, 'Well, what happened, preacher?' I'll tell you what happened. Chapter nineteen, verse twenty-four."

I turned the tissue-thin pages of the bible to chapter nineteen and scanned the numbered verses until I found twenty-four.

The preacher shuffled his feet and leaned over the podium, his breathing amplified by the microphone. "Then the Lord rained upon Sodom and upon Gomorrah brimstone and fire."

Louder cries of "That's right!" and "Yes!" rang out from the congregation.

Brother O'Dell continued his tirade on the sinfulness of homosexuality. To prove my innocence, I tried to maintain eye contact with him as he cited various passages that not only condemned gays, but justified their execution.

He quoted Leviticus 20:13: "If a man also lie with mankind as he lieth with a woman, both of them have committed an abomination. They shall surely be put to death. Their blood shall be upon them."

I swallowed hard and hung my head, hoping no one would notice the sweat rolling off me, pooling in my armpits and the small of my back. My mouth felt dry.

The preacher moved on to First Corinthians. "Chapter six, verse nine and ten: 'Know ye not that the unrighteous shall not inherit the kingdom of God. Be not deceived. Neither fornicators nor idolaters, nor adulterers, nor effeminate, nor abusers of themselves with mankind, nor thieves, nor covetous, nor drunkards, nor revilers, nor extortioners shall inherit the kingdom of God.'"

Brother O'Dell shook his finger at us—seemingly at me. "Buddy, you better not be deceived."

I glanced at Mom, who was apparently reading the entire book of Leviticus while fanning herself with the Christian magazine she got in Sunday school class. I never considered the apprehension she must have been feeling about being divorced, which the preacher had said many times was equivalent to adultery. She and my dad had divorced when I was two, after having been married for twenty years and having six children together. A few years later, she married John Riggs. It was my stepfather's death in an accident on the railroad tracks the year before that had brought us to Belmont Baptist Church.

John Riggs was ten years younger than Mom, and he had three kids of his own, but didn't see them much due to a bitter divorce. I was the youngest of six. My siblings were older and already on their own, for the most part. When I was nine years old, my youngest sister, Violet, got married, and I officially became the only child left in the household.

On January 28, 1979, when I was ten, John was feeling ill, and we had to go to the pharmacy in Shepherdsville to pick up a prescription for him. It was frigid that Sunday, and the sky was winter gray. We left home around noon, right as church services were letting out at Belmont Baptist. There was snow on the ground. John was driving. When we got to the railroad crossing, the front wheel of our rust-brown Pontiac LeMans got stuck in a pothole. John got out and started pushing.

Suddenly, l heard a train whistle blasting like a weeping elephant, and John was yelling, "Jump, honey! Jump!"

But Mom froze, as though locked up by the cold, and the train's engine smashed into the front of our car, knocking us off the tracks and hurling us several hundred feet.

The impact had stunned me, and perhaps my mother. I'm not sure how much time passed before we gathered our bearings and crawled from the wreckage in the snow along the side of the tracks. I remember seeing a silver disk resting on a pristine space of slushy white ground, and on closer inspection, saw that it was a dime, I knew instantly that it had flown out of Mom's purse. The rest of the contents were strewn in the snow. We would later learn that the eyeglasses she was wearing had flown in another direction, into the back dash behind me.

As we got to our feet, we began yelling for John. He never responded. We rounded the crumpled LeMans and found him lying face up on the ground, half his body under the wreckage. His eyes were open and eager, as though waiting for assistance, but when Mom pulled on his arm to help him up, his head collapsed, exposing the bloody contents. Mom began screaming hysterically and shaking her hands as if they had caught on fire. For some reason, I took off down the tracks toward home to call someone. I wasn't sure who, but going home and calling someone was the only thing I could think of to do. However, Mom called me back, and some of our neighbors arrived and ushered us the other way, across the tracks and down onto Church Avenue, where an old lady was standing on her porch in a long floral-print muumuu. She waved us inside and put us in the front sitting room. Someone called the police. I watched out the front window until the ambulance pulled up.

The authorities told us that John had died instantly, and that he hadn't felt any pain in the accident. It was a long ambulance ride to the hospital in Louisville, but Mom and I were released the same day. Mom was in shock and heavily medicated. I had suffered some bruises on my face, but nothing significant. We were treated and released that same day. When we got out, my main goal was seeing what the eleven o'clock news would report about us. I had learned well how to hide my feelings, how to divert my attention from whatever hurt me. I could not fathom, at the time, that John was gone forever, could not fathom the grief that would swallow my mother.

After the wreck, Mom could not bring herself to return to the house in Belmont, so we stayed across the county with my sister Myrtle for three months, and I changed schools. Not long after we finally moved back home, Mom started attending Sunday morning services at Belmont Baptist Church. I don't recall the pastor visiting or women from the church calling to invite her, although that might have happened. She may have gotten a card in the mail, or a push from one of our neighbors. But what I do remember is my mother being lost after John died. The world went quiet that winter, and our family drifted uneasily for about a year. And after that, I started going to church, too.

***

As Brother Larry led the closing prayer, I inched my way to the end of the pew, preparing for my escape. There was no way to avoid shaking hands with Brother O'Dell, who stood just outside the vestibule expressly for that purpose. Everyone else seemed to look up to him, clamoring on the church steps to have a word with him about the sermon or the next gospel singing, or to suggest an activity for vacation bible school. I didn't understand their admiration. I had no inclination to fellowship that way. I could not shake off the preacher's judgmental words and the pain they caused me, especially that day. It was not enough to suffer the heat of the sanctuary for an hour and a half, to be condemned to hell, sentenced to execution. I was expected to show respect, and for my mother's sake, I did.

Afterward, I felt dirty. Then I raced through the gravel lot to our dusty green Oldsmobile and waited. The interior was so hot I could hardly breathe. I left the passenger door open and slumped down in the seat, quietly whimpering until Mom got into the car and drove us home.

***

Six years later, I escaped the oppressive beliefs of that pastor and found a community a hundred miles away at Berea College, where Christianity meant service to others and loving your neighbor. The atmosphere there gave me a sense of purpose and the hope that I could accomplish some good in the world.

I had not yet come out as gay when I graduated, moved back home, and started working as a registered nurse in the Open Heart Unit at Audubon Hospital in Louisville. However, my four years at Berea had given me the courage to trust my gut—where, I found, the voice of God dwelled—on matters of the heart.

"You need to relax and take a load off," my coworker suggested.

Like myself, Stan was a recent graduate and also new to the profession. We were sitting at the nurses' station at Audubon working on patient charts. Earlier he had noticed me taking the small print information pamphlets from the medications and studying them to better understand pharmacokinetics. I had been focusing all my energy on my job, immersing myself in learning about the high-tech medical equipment we used to save patients' lives. I was fascinated with the heart as the body's most vital organ, and I subconsciously allowed that fascination to occupy my time, diverting attention from my personal desires—in particular, my attraction to men, which I'd been telling myself since I was ten years old was just a phase I was going through.

I glanced up at Stan and smiled. "I'm fine," I said. "I'm just getting started. There's so much to learn. I think it's exciting."

"You need a break," he insisted. "And I think I know just the place."

I laughed. "Cancun, right?"

He waved a hand at me. "You don't have time for that. No vacation time yet. But seriously, you should check out this place downtown called The Connection. It's on South Floyd Street."

My heart thudded in my chest. I had somehow heard of that nightclub. It was a gay bar. I didn't let on that I knew, but I had to wonder whether Stan was on to me. He knew I had been dating Lisa, who was also a nurse, for the past couple months.

During college, I had worked hard to overcome the "phase." I had dated girls during most of my college career, but the relationships were very superficial and lasted only until things got serious, which was my cue to somehow sabotage the romance. I must have realized that the "phase" wasn't a phase at all, but a permanent trait, and so I stopped short of committing to a long-term affair. This way I kept myself from getting into a situation that could lead to marriage and children.

I tried to sound casual asking Stan about The Connection "What's so great about this place?"

He ran a hand through his dark hair and adjusted his glasses. "Good music, fun entertainment. The drinks. The people."

I nodded and watched him for a moment while he reviewed some notes. Stan had been to the club himself. I eyed his starkly white shoes, considered his demeanor, and suddenly I understood that his suggestion had nothing to do with me and everything to do with him. *Of course! Stan is gay,* I thought.

I chuckled. "I can't call in sick to go to a bar. I'd be putting my job in jeopardy."

He shrugged. "Happens all the time in this line of work. This is a hospital. People get sick. Trust me."

I stopped and looked over at him. "You really think I should go to this place? Alone?"

"Most definitely alone," he recommended. "It's a singles kind of place." He winked and grinned at me.

* * *

I didn't think about going to The Connection again until the next evening, around the time I would normally get ready for work.

I had moved back home with my mom and her new husband, Otis, from the church, and after rolling out of bed about three PM, I spent the first part of my day catching up with them. When John died, Mom had found it too difficult to live in the same house, so we had bought a trailer and moved it next door, and started renting the old house to a local family. As soon as I graduated college, we broke ground on a new house on the same lot with the trailer. After breakfast, I checked out the work that the contractors had completed and worked for a few hours to fill in some of the gaps left between construction crews.

It was a spur of the moment decision to call in sick. Mom and Otis were winding down watching TV, and I was wide awake and ready to try something new. I wasn't worried about Lisa, the nurse I was dating. We had a casual relationship, and I knew I would be ending it before long.

I took a shower and got dressed. Before I could talk myself out of it, I grabbed my wallet and my keys and told Mom I was going out.

The sun had already set by the time I got to the bar, but I was still nervous about being seen. I parked my car in a lot a block away and walked to the canopied entrance.

The exterior looked like any other building on South Floyd, a dull, grayish industrial structure with a few tiny windows. As I approached it, I resisted the urge to turn around and see whether anyone was watching me. The closer I got to the entrance, the more my stomach fluttered and the faster my heart raced.

I stepped inside, paid my cover charge, and walked into a thick cloud of cigarette smoke. It took a minute for my eyes to adjust. At first, I had the sensation of being in a haunted house. I knew there would be some kind of show, but I had no idea what it would involve, and I was frightened in that childlike way, anticipating the unknown. This was new territory for me. I had never even seen two guys kiss in real life.

In that soup of emotions, I was also terrified of being spotted here by someone who knew me, terrified of the repercussions of being seen. I had thought I would leave that feeling at the door, but in the dizzying swirl of disco lights, I felt it more intensely. All the bullying of my childhood and teen years rushed back to me for those first minutes. I was afraid of hurting that way again. I would have rather felt the sting of a slap or the crush of a fist against my jaw than experience that kind of torment. I did not know the intentions of any of these people, but I knew how rumors spread and the way gossip worked.

I followed the music—the jangly beat of INXS's "New Sensation" so loud I could feel the bass thumping inside me—to a black-and-white checkered dance floor. A sea of bodies moved under flashing multicolored lights, all arms and wild hair and the kind of shiny metallic shirts and skirts that were popular back then. There were male couples, female couples, male-female couples, and some who were indistinguishable, which made me smile; here was a place for everyone, I thought, and some of my anxiety melted away.

Across from the dance floor was a small piano bar where a few couples sat chatting on couches, sipping drinks from sleek cocktail glasses. Beyond the piano bar was the show bar, where a drag show was in progress. The walls were lined with floor-to-ceiling mirrors, and I checked my hair as I entered to make sure it looked okay. The room was crowded with couples and small groups. I felt a bit awkward, so I stood alone on the perimeter next to the cigarette machine to watch the show.

A bevy of cheers went up for each performer who took the stage. Each wore a seductive costume with sequins and came out draped in veils or other loose garments that were slowly stripped away. They marched across the stage in fishnet hose, and their routines were well timed and rehearsed. Many of them would have passed for beautiful women on the street. Their bodies were lean and well toned, shapely and feminine in every way. Perhaps that's why, again and again, my eyes were drawn back to their faces, where, beneath the lipstick and heavy eyeliner, I could detect at least a hint of maleness.

I knew what attracted me: masculine, athletic men. I had no sooner silently affirmed my tastes when my eye caught precisely the type of man I liked. And it seemed to be just my luck that the best-looking guy in the bar was already engaged in conversation with another man. I kept watching him anyway, and eventually he must have felt my eyes on him because he turned and looked over at me. I smiled as handsomely as possible, every muscle in my mouth aching from the strain of it. He flashed a quick grin and resumed conversation with his friend. I hoped that was all it was, a friendship. They were just talking, not holding hands or kissing like some of the other couples. I stayed close to the cigarette machine on the off chance it might be true.

A few minutes later, the handsome guy walked toward me. He was wearing snug-fitting jeans and a short-sleeved gingham shirt that showed off his biceps; even fully dressed, his sporty physique was obvious. As he passed, he nodded.

"Hello," I said, and I was thankful when he paused. I couldn't take my eyes off him. "What's your name?" I asked.

When his eyes met mine, the wings of a thousand butterflies unfurled in my belly, and I felt a bit faint. Was this really happening to me?

"Paul," he said. "What's yours?"

"Randy," I replied. "Randy Johnson."

He squinted at me. "Really?"

I laughed, wondering what his point was. "Yes, really!" I exclaimed. I offered to show him my license.

He shook his head and smiled. "Never mind. It just sounded ... I don't know. Like you're incognito."

I was so amused and dazzled by him, I felt giddy. I kept thinking how lucky I was to have met this sweet, brown-eyed hunk. *Paul.* I repeated his name in my head so I wouldn't forget. There was something different about his accent. "Where are you from?" I asked.

"New York, actually," he said.

I could only think of skyscrapers crammed together, traffic jams and taxi drivers laying on their horns, and sidewalks crowded enough to make pick-pocketing a profession.

Paul was glancing around the show bar. "Should we get a table?"

"I'd love to," I responded. "But what about your friend?"

"That's my brother, Mike. He lives here in town. I've been visiting him this week."

I breathed a sigh of relief. "I can't tell you how glad I am to hear that."

Paul blushed and his eyes fell to the checkered dance floor. His shyness sparked something in me—a deepened sense of affection for him, an urge to protect him from those who might take advantage of his unassuming nature.

We got a couple beers and found a small table in a spot where we could talk above the music and noise of patrons. In any other situation, I might have balked at the folding metal chairs, the same kind used for seating at wedding receptions and family reunions. But with Paul seated across from me, it didn't matter. I probably would have sat on a pile of rocks for the chance to have a conversation with him.

I leaned on the table, focusing all my attention on him, and propped my chin in the palm of my hand. "Tell me about yourself. Do you go to gay bars back home?"

He fidgeted with his beer, turning the bottle, and nodded. "I've been to a few, but it always feels risky, like I could get in trouble for being there. What about you?"

"That's exactly how I felt about coming here tonight!" I exclaimed, and I took a swig of my beer. "I was so nervous. This is my first time."

Paul pouted sympathetically. He glanced around and shrugged. "It's not so bad for me right now since I don't know any of these people, and it's highly unlikely any of them know me."

It hit me then. In the few minutes we had been talking, much of my fear had dissipated. At that moment, all that mattered to me was getting to know this man. I might have even had the nerve to get up on stage to win his affection, if that's what it took. Thankfully, I didn't have to. Paul was kind and attentive, and our conversation progressed easily from personal life to work life to family.

Like me, he was the youngest in a large family and sort of a mama's boy. I learned that he had struggled most of his life with his sexuality, which was also familiar to me, but unlike me, he had come out to family and friends. While some relationships were lost in the process, he said others had grown and flourished. His parents, who were devout Catholics, had taken the news badly, which had caused a rift among his siblings that troubled Paul immensely.

"We've always been close," he said. "It's been very painful to lose their companionship."

I shook my head. "I couldn't imagine what it would be like to be separated from my family. They mean the world to me."

"I agree," Paul said. "Love is what holds a family together, and that love should be strong enough to survive anything. I feel it for them in every respect. Unconditionally. That's what families are for."

He had articulated my exact feelings. I stared at him in amazement. I'm sure my jaw was hanging open.

He beamed at me and raised his beer. "To families?"

"Yes! To families!"

We drained our bottles and before we could order another, Paul's brother apologetically interrupted our conversation. He acknowledged me with a nod and turned to Paul. "I'm getting bored. Think I'll head home."

Paul and I looked at each other. I was desperate not to lose his company. "I could drive you back myself," I offered.

"That would be great," Paul said cheerfully, grinning and lacing his fingers together on the table as though he had just won a round of poker.

"It's in Prospect," Mike informed me, and he scribbled some directions on a napkin. I thanked him, and we watched him exit the room before resuming our conversation.

"So what's it like living in New York?" I asked. "Seems like it would be crazy with the traffic and all the people."

"Not where I'm from," Paul said. "I live in Western New York, clear across the state. We have dairy farms and grape vineyards. The Big Apple's six hours away."

"Is that where you teach, Western New York?" I asked. I could easily picture him in a teaching role. He seemed patient and caring.

"Yeah, in a city called Jamestown. About seventy miles south of Buffalo."

"Do you like teaching?"

Paul smiled wistfully, and I knew the answer before he said it. "Very much so. The kids are great. I'd love to have kids of my own one day."

"So would I. But what are the chances of that?"

Paul held his chin in his hand and thought for a moment. "Anything is possible."

I loved his attitude and his determination.

"When do you go back?" I wanted to know. "To New York, I mean."

He frowned and wilted a little, and again I guessed his response before he spoke, and knew it would not be in my favor. "Tomorrow."

My stomach sank, a hollow space collapsing inside me, while Paul's gaze drifted off across the room, his face bathed in neon. But when I reached across the table, his hand opened to mine, and I squeezed his palm and swallowed back my tears. When I was able to speak, I told him that I hoped we could stay in touch. "I don't know if it's too early to say this, but I feel a special connection with you. I've never felt that before."

"I feel it, too," he said. "We have to stay in touch." His gentle eyes waited for mine before he added, "I wouldn't have it any other way."

After a four-hour conversation, we walked to my car. We sat in the dark interior of my 1989 Ford Mustang listening to the radio for a few minutes. The Bryan Adams song "Everything I Do, I Do for You" was playing, and the words hit me with a strange force.

Look into my eyes,
You will see
What you mean to me ...
Search your heart,
Search your soul
And when you find me there, you'll search no more ...
Don't tell me it's not worth tryin' for
You can't tell me it's not worth dyin' for...

"Good song," Paul said, and just the way he said it gave me courage, as though he was agreeing with the crooner on the radio, and before I could think twice, I asked if I could kiss him. It was impulsive and out of character for me. I had been an introvert my entire life and had never initiated a move that romantic, that intimate. And never before with another man. Even before Paul consented, I started to feel jittery. Could I pull this off? I wondered. My heart was pounding out of my chest.

But when he said yes, I didn't waste any time leaning in close to him, breathing in the heady scent of his cologne and the mild, yeasty odor of our beer breath as our mouths met. Our lips pressed together, tongues slowly touching, and our bodies fused like two lost pieces of a puzzle we'd been trying to build our whole lives. I wished that kiss would never end.

For the next six months, the memory of that night would sustain me for every obstacle I had yet to overcome.

6: The Storm

Paul

Dr. Bell was a University of Louisville fan. That alone might have been enough to seal the deal. But on top of that, he treated Randy and me like we were any other couple. Our conversation progressed easily from robotic medical technology to sports. We talked basketball like old college friends.

When the biopsy results came back, I had wanted to look at every angle, to explore every possibility for ridding my body of the cancer in the most effective way with the fewest side effects. After that first visit with Dr. Bell, I was certain I'd found the answer. I was convinced the da Vinci prostatectomy was the way to go. Dr. Bell made the surgery sound routine, and his confidence in its success gave me confidence. Randy and I left his office knowing that we would be calling to schedule the surgery as soon as I could figure out my schedule for the rest of the academic year.

That same day, I had an appointment, scheduled several weeks earlier, to discuss treatment options with a radiation oncologist. It was too late to cancel, so Randy and I decided to drive back across the bridge into downtown Louisville, grab some lunch, and head to Suburban Hospital, where the doctor's office was located, on the east side of town.

It had started out a typical spring day in Kentucky, although spring wouldn't officially begin for another three weeks. The dogwoods had yet to bloom, but the turf around the city was beginning to thicken. A few lazy clouds drifted across the pale blue sky, occasionally blotting out the sun, but as we exited the parking lot, its light glared against the glass medical complex, and the building glowed in an oddly beautiful way, as though it held some sort of secret treasure.

Randy checked a message on his phone and grunted. "That's strange." He leaned on the steering wheel and scanned the horizon. "It's a weather alert."

I turned on the radio and changed channels until I heard some mention of the weather. Randy turned up the volume.

"An intense storm system is heading our way.... Right now it's affecting the Great Lakes region north of us, and it's beginning to move across the Ohio Valley .... We're under a severe thunderstorm and a tornado watch right now, but that's likely to be upgraded as the day progresses. The National Weather Service says we're facing a high risk of severe weather over the next twenty-four hours, including tornadoes ... in Louisville and surrounding areas ... with the worst of the impact expected to hit later this afternoon. There have already been reports of tornado touchdowns in Indiana. We'll keep you updated as reports come in."

Randy and I looked at each other. "We better let the kids know," I suggested. We were off school that day, and we had left Tevin in charge at home.

"Yeah," Randy agreed, and he made the call while we were stopped at a traffic light. "Tev, the weather's supposed to get bad, and we've got another doctor appointment to go to. Keep the TV on and check the reports. If it starts to get bad, round up your sister and brothers and get everybody down to the basement."

I could hear Tevin's muffled voice responding. I imagined he was looking out the window and doubting the forecast.

Randy was nodding, trying not to interrupt Tevin's assessment of the situation. "They're saying storms are moving in later this afternoon, but we're under a tornado watch now, so you guys need to be on alert."

Randy was firm, but I wished he would be firmer. I worried that the kids would go back to their video games or their movies and totally forget about what was going on outdoors. I pressed my fist to my mouth, a gesture I normally used to stifle a cough, and resisted the urge to tell Randy how to handle the kids. Instead, I searched the sky for any clues of ominous weather. It was hard to believe tornadoes were heading our way. I couldn't blame Tevin for his skepticism.

I found the weather an interesting parallel to my condition, how I looked and felt healthy, but within my prostate gland, cancer was growing. Malignancy. A scourge. A curse. A growth that would destroy my body if left untreated, that could lead to an outbreak—high winds and hail and a deluge of cancerous cells spreading through lymph nodes and blood and bone, leaving a trail of destruction. I wanted to grab the phone from Randy and relay this analogy to Tevin. Looks can be deceiving. A storm could be brewing; a microscopic cancer could be hiding in wait. I couldn't tell which was making me more anxious—the weather forecast or my health crisis.

It was still sunny and warm when we arrived at Suburban Hospital. We parked in the garage and took the elevator to the lower level, which was both a blessing and a curse. While we were relieved to be in the safest space in the building, there were no windows for us to see what was happening outside. To make matters worse, as I signed in, I noticed that the nurses and assistants were all talking about the approaching storm. The receptionist was calling patients to cancel afternoon appointments, and a few others were on their cell phones advising coworkers against coming in.

"We're closing up early," said one of the callers, who stood behind the reception desk in pink scrubs with one hand on her hip, her face grim.

The receptionist paused from her phone conversation to check my name. She gave me a quick smile. "You can have a seat, sir. We'll get you in in just a few minutes."

When I sat down, Randy was checking weather reports on his phone. He pointed at the nearly empty room, where two or three other people were waiting to be seen. "Shouldn't be long," he muttered, without taking his eyes off his phone.

On the TV in the waiting area, an emergency weather bulletin rolled across the bottom of the screen. I folded my arms across my chest. "I'm worried about the kids."

"They're fine, Dad. The storm's not even close."

"Is that what it says on the Weather Channel?"

"We have some time. They're saying later this afternoon."

"But we should call and check on them."

Randy was already dialing the phone. He spoke to Tevin. "You all should probably head down to the basement. Dad's worried." He winked at me.

"It's a severe storm," I shot back. "I just want them to be safe."

Randy gave me a thumbs up while he listened to Tevin. "Get the flashlights, and make sure they have batteries in them. And make sure there's water and whatever down there in the fridge. We'll be there in an hour or two." He paused, pressing his ear against the receiver. "What?"

I thought something was wrong until he rolled his eyes. "Yes, we'll stop and pick up something to eat on the way home."

I chuckled. "Can't survive a storm without food."

A few minutes later, the assistant in pink scrubs called us back and led us to a simple office with a desk and two chairs. I wondered instantly whether the oncologist expected opposite genders to be seated in those chairs, whether he would deny me medical advice because of my sexual orientation. This was always the most stressful part of the visit—pondering the physician's receptiveness to the fact that we were gay and his or her willingness to recognize us as a couple. Even though I had already made up my mind about having the surgery, the thought of rejection by this doctor, or any doctor for that matter, troubled me. It hurt to be looked on as inferior. It hurt to be assessed unfavorably because of who you loved.

The doctor stepped in a few minutes later. He was a small Asian man with dark hair, and I sensed right away that he had a keen sensibility. He introduced himself and went straight to work explaining my options for radiation treatment: seed implantation and direct radiation; the latter would require me to be seen three times a week. He explained the benefits and the risks, which we already knew.

"I take it that you have explored other possible treatments?" he asked.

"Yes," I replied. "In fact, we saw a surgeon this morning—Dr. Bell—about a prostatectomy using the da Vinci procedure, and I feel fairly confident that's the route I'm going to take."

"I understand, and that's good," the doctor said. "Dr. Bell is highly renowned in his field."

I appreciated his tact and professionalism, and the impartial way he handled the conversation seeing that we were a couple. In the end, I was glad we'd had the chance to talk to him, but I was eager to head home and be with my family. The doctor seemed attuned to my sense of urgency, although he might have attributed it more to the cancer than to the approaching storm. He closed the folder on his desk and asked whether we had any questions.

"I think you covered everything," I replied. "We appreciate your time."

He stood up and offered his hand. "I hope your surgery goes well," he said, sincerity showing in his eyes and the firmness of his grip.

"Thank you so much," I said, returning a brief but sturdy grasp before moving toward the door.

Over my shoulder, I watched Randy shake his hand and was warmed by the interaction, the simple kindness shown to us. Was it really that hard to accept who we were? Occasions such as this buoyed me up, proving how easy it could be, giving me faith that the world could change.

By the time we left Suburban, the wind had already picked up. We could tell when we stepped off the elevator into the parking garage. Gusts of wind swirled in the gaps between levels, stirring an empty soda bottle and a few bits of trash that whizzed up in the air and fluttered to the ground like paper kamikaze airplanes. When we drove out of the parking garage, the skies had grown dark; the trees were bowing and the power lines along the streets were swaying.

We listened to the radio and kept an eye on the skies, stopping at a drive-thru to pick up food.

"You know, we're either really bad parents or really good parents, depending on how you look at it," Randy said, reaching for his wallet as he pulled up to the window.

I allowed myself to laugh a little. "I know." I glanced at the clock. "We have time to make it home."

Although we were making light of the matter, the issue of bad parenting had cropped up repeatedly over the years. We had grown used to the stares, the impolite gestures, and the spoken and unspoken suggestions of others who doubted our ability as gay men to properly raise children. The fact that people were watching and judging us added another layer of tension to the normal challenges of parenthood— juggling childcare, dealing with sibling rivalry, addressing homework and hygiene. On top of that, we had to coach our kids on handling mistreatment because of their skin color and having two dads. We were constantly vigilant of living in this fishbowl.

Randy drove a little too fast on the way home, but I said nothing to stop him. Ominous clouds were roiling above us, and pink and white flashes flared in the skyline behind us over downtown Louisville. I realized when we turned into our subdivision that my shoulders were stiff with tension, and I rubbed the back of my neck.

"You okay, Dad?" Randy caressed my shoulder.

I patted his hand. "Yeah, it's just been a crazy day." I blew out my breath.

"But it was a good day," he proposed. "Don't you think?"

I hadn't given much thought to the actual surgery. The weather had been a welcome diversion and, at the same time, an appropriate metaphor for the turbulent conditions I was up against. I'd spent the last few hours in a fierce fight with the elements to ensure our children would be safe and out of harm's way. On another level, I needed the same kind of strength and stamina to get through the storm of this surgery and back to the family I cherished, to help protect them from the prejudices that we came up against daily.

Randy had shut off the engine and was waiting for my response.

I handed him the drink carrier and grabbed the white bags from the floorboard. "I really like Dr. Bell. I have a good feeling about him. But, you know, surgery is scary, and cancer is even scarier."

"It's all going to be fine," Randy insisted.

I let the conversation rest on that note. I loved his optimism, but the truth of the matter was that everything would not be fine. The truth was we were caught in an endless tempest. It wasn't just the cancer or the surgery. We had no idea how the hospital staff would respond to our situation, if they would give us the same rights as other couples for visitation, if they would allow everyone to participate as a family member in my treatment and recovery. And of course, there were all the other implications that Randy and I had discussed repeatedly since the twins were born—the legal rights, the financial insecurities, everything we risked losing if one of us became disabled or died. It was a nightmare to think about, let alone talk about. We had talked it to death. There were no solutions, only anger and frustration over the situation.

The food was still warm as we carried it into the kitchen, where the kids let out a gigantic "Hooray!" not only because we had arrived safely, but because we came bearing gifts of burgers and fries.

Tevin doled out the sandwiches and sides, and we ate in a chaotic manner, without saying grace or all of us sitting down at the table. The TV was on, and warnings were announced for neighborhoods west of us. Kenzie forgot something in her bedroom and trotted up the stairs. Tevin and Tyler were checking out a weather map online and gauging the strength of the storm. Randy and DeSean had stepped out onto the deck and were watching cloud formations.

I opened the back door and called out to them. "It's getting really close. We need to go to the basement."

The trees were whipping in the wind. Thunder rumbled from one side of the darkened sky to the other.

"We're coming," Randy assured me.

I retreated inside and ushered Tevin, Tyler, and Kenzie downstairs.

Just as hail began hitting the walkout patio, Randy and DeSean came barreling down the basement steps.

"Thank God," I breathed.

We gathered in the TV room, but Randy was drawn to the patio, where evidence of the storm's power was plainly visible. Eventually, he gave up the dangerous spectacle of lightning, hail, and high winds, and settled down with us to wait out the storm. The worst of it was over half an hour later. Before bed, we heard reports of death and devastation in several states. Among the hardest hit areas was Henryville, Indiana, where the town's elementary and junior high schools suffered extensive damage; amazingly, no one in either building was killed, and only minor injuries were reported. The news was chilling.

A few days later, while making dinner, we saw a TV report on the evening news of a Henryville woman who had lost both legs protecting her children from one of the many tornados that ravaged our region that day. The mother, Stephanie Decker, explained that there had been no time to prepare and no place to go, so she wrapped the children in a blanket and lay on top of them while the tornado raged over them. A steel beam had crashed down on the three of them. Although the children were not physically harmed, the mother's legs were crushed.

The report filmed Decker as she was leaving U of L hospital in a wheelchair. I could not imagine the terror of the ordeal and the despair I would feel over losing my legs, yet Stephanie Decker said she felt lucky to be alive. She was humble about her heroic action and upbeat about returning to her family.

I wanted to cry—for the intense love of this woman and the example she set, and for my selfish and petty concerns over surgery to have my prostate removed. What I was going through was nothing in the face of what this mother had survived. I thought of all the suffering that resulted from the outbreak—the forty-one deaths, the thousands of homes that were lost, the nightmares of children forever changed by the experience.

That night before bed, I prayed for forgiveness. *Lord, help me to appreciate the blessing of every day, every hour, every minute. Amen.*

7: Dressing Room Blues

Randy

I t was early spring, not long after Paul's diagnosis, and Mackenzie had a dance competition at Memorial Auditorium, an old concert hall in downtown Louisville. The day of the event, the dance moms and I arrived early and crammed into the dressing room backstage with costumes and accessories. We shepherded the girls into separate spaces along the walls and corners, the way we usually did, and began helping our daughters change. They ranged in age from about seven to twelve, so they counted on us parents to help them keep up with the nonstop competition schedule. I was careful to respect the privacy of the others, keeping my back to them and my focus on Kenzie. We made adjustments and touched up makeup until the last possible minute when the girls were called to the stage, then we followed them out the door to the wings, where we could catch the highlights of each number before rushing backstage for the next change.

I peeked out at the audience and saw Paul in the crowd cheering and clapping wildly as the girls took their positions on stage. I couldn't help but grin at him.

One of the moms noticed and nudged me, winking. "You two are such good dads," she said.

"Just blessed to get to be dads," I replied, and turned to watch the girls' jazz routine.

It seemed time had stopped after Paul's diagnosis. For several weeks, nothing else had mattered in that great void. I'd lost interest in everything and turned my attention solely to him and his needs— gathering insurance information and medical documents, getting professional opinions, researching treatment options, making appointments. We'd had several long, honest conversations in the privacy of our bedroom that ended the same way—with Paul insisting that we carry on as normal, that we focus on our family, that we live in the moment and make the most of every day.

"The kids still need us, especially Kenzie. Kenzie really needs us to be there for her," he had reasoned.

How could I disagree? Yet I was afraid to go on—to move forward. I understood then that it wasn't time that had stopped, it was me. I was stuck. I was scared. Through every pep talk I'd given Paul, I was trying to convince myself that everything was going to be okay. I knew he was right about holding fast and forging ahead, and I loved him for it. I loved him for his devotion to our children, his steady mind, and his selflessness, which, although often at the root of our discord, precisely defined the man I loved.

Kenzie was in third grade at the Brown School. She was a happy and confident eight year old, and we owed much of that to her four years as a student at Dancensation, the local studio where she had advanced from the ranks of "tiny tapper" to more serious classes in jazz and ballet. Kenzie thrived on the attention she got from performing, and she worked hard to earn her turn in the spotlight, immersing herself in rehearsals and routines while winning the respect and friendship of the other girls.

We'd heard about Dancensation through a friend when Tyler and Tevin expressed an interest in learning dance in eighth grade. Although Tevin bowed out after six months, Tyler flourished on stage, and Kenzie looked to him for inspiration and encouragement. Participating in dance gave both of them something to focus their energy on while teaching them to appreciate the artistic and competitive merits of performance. Paul and I had mandated the kids to take part in some type of extracurricular activity, whether it involved sports, music, or art, and Tyler and Kenzie seemed to find their niche in the performing arts. We were pleased that they had, for the most part, discovered and pursued these interests on their own, and we were determined to do whatever necessary to ensure they had a positive experience. This meant keeping a close watch out for intolerant attitudes and biased behavior around our kids.

Thankfully, the environment at Dancensation had turned out to be open and accepting, and I had quickly befriended the group of moms who sat watching their daughters and sons practice while sharing advice and information on everything dance-related. My fellow "dance moms" had taught me the importance of using Velcro to modify costumes, and I had suggested new hairstyles—such as braids in lieu of straightened hair—that gave the girls an innovative look while complimenting my daughter's natural features. The mothers praised my braid and bead work and other hairstyles I did on Kenzie that were sheer experimental efforts with good results. I learned how to wield a curling iron, attach bows, apply hairspray, and make other uses of hair products—such as dabbing gel on Kenzie's eyelids, tilting her head back, and sprinkling glitter over her closed eyes. The mothers and I had become a tight-knit group working together to support our children, provide transportation to and from events, and assist backstage when needed.

Paul had no interest in taking on these duties and was more apt to sit in the truck until class was over than mingle with the moms. I felt compelled to fill the need for Kenzie, mainly because I didn't want her experience to be different from the other girls', and I also didn't want the other parents or girls pitying her because she didn't have a mother. I wanted to prove that, regardless of my gender, I could assist my daughter with any need and could nurture her femininity as well as her fortitude.

Early on, I had told the school's owner, Sandra Rivera, "I assure you that Mackenzie will never suffer because she doesn't have a mom. I will work as hard as I possibly can to keep her from feeling slighted or embarrassed about having a dad where the other girls have moms."

Sandra's face had brightened, and she had patted my arm encouragingly. "I'm sure you will, and we will do our best to support you."

As the girls grew older and started performing more complex routines with costume changes between acts, I had joined the other mothers in the dressing room. It had happened quite naturally with no resistance from any of the girls or the mothers. Sandra required all students, male and female, to wear a tan bodysuit as a base layer beneath their costume for everyone's comfort and security. The bodysuit stayed on through all costume changes.

All this had worked well until a new student joined the ranks. Lola was a year or two older than the other girls and more mature physically, which resulted in a troublesome situation at the spring competition.

When the jazz number was over, the moms and I hurried back to the dressing room and prepared for the onslaught of girls flinging off scarves and other garments as they trotted to their spaces. Kenzie kicked off her shoes and reached for her new outfit, which I held out for her. It was four minutes of chaos, slipping into clothes and shoes, fixing hair, and applying makeup or glitter.

I was putting Kenzie's hair into a ponytail when I noticed Lola and her mother Suzie motionless next to us. I glanced only long enough to see Lola snatching her garments from Suzie's arms and spinning around to face the wall, and I hastily averted my gaze, concentrating on the ponytail holder, then tugging Kenzie's tutu into place. Next thing I knew, Suzie was beside me, arms crossed defensively, her face stern, and I knew the conversation was going to be ugly.

She modulated her voice as though trying to keep from creating a scene, yet clearly and slowly enunciated every word. "My daughter is not comfortable with you being in the dressing room."

My face felt hot but I did not look away, instead fixing my eyes on hers and waiting a minute for a reasonable response to come to me. As much as I wanted to shout at her, I resisted. I patted Kenzie on the back and steered her away from the confrontation.

Suzie blinked and frowned at me, which I took as a subtle warning. "I can't have this. I'm sorry. It's just wrong."

I wasn't prepared for her brazenness. "What? You think it's wrong for me to be here to support my daughter the same way you're supporting yours?"

"Daddy, can I—"

I waved her off. "Not now, Kenzie."

Suzie folded her arms over her chest. "It's wrong for a man to be in the dressing room with a bunch of young girls." Her eyes darted around the room.

For a second I realized everyone was watching. I stood my ground. "We're not leaving."

"Oh, come on. You can't be serious. You're a man." She threw out her hands and glared at me, then lowered her voice and tried another tack. "Lola's very self-conscious about her body. She started her menstrual cycle. She's a woman now. I don't think you understand. It's nothing personal—"

"But it is personal," I interrupted. "You're personally rooting me out and asking me to sacrifice my daughter's right to have a parent present when your daughter is the one who's uncomfortable. If she's uncomfortable, then you'll have to find another dressing room to go to. I'm not doing that to my daughter."

Suzie's lips tightened and her face flushed with anger. Just when I thought she was about to offer a retort, she spun on her heels and stormed off.

Suddenly one of the parents called out from the hallway, "We're up next!"

Kenzie gazed up at me, dark, wondering eyes peering out from spidery lashes, then dashed out the door with the other girls.

***

Contrary to what some people expected, Paul and I did not cast ourselves into gender roles, with one of us acting as the father while the other methodically tended to the tasks of motherhood. We saw ourselves as equal contributors in the childrearing process. For example, I was the one who taught the kids practical life skills, like mowing the lawn and learning to drive the car, while Paul focused on getting them to do daily routines such as homework and hygiene.

Our decision to adopt a baby girl had been carefully deliberated. We had considered what we could offer—love, stability, a home, a family—and felt those were the most critical components in a child's upbringing. We had proven ourselves capable with the boys, who were healthy, well mannered, and successful in school.

We talked at length about adding a daughter to our household—about how it would diversify our worldview and that of our sons, as well as even out Paul's and my parental authority, since I would be the one to legally adopt her. Although we considered each other equal halves, I often felt excluded when it came to official business involving the boys, such as when certain school papers needed signed or the official parent had to make a formal decision about something. I was eager to expand our family and strike that unusual balance of power that other families never had to worry about.

A couple months after the twins' eighth birthday, we contacted the adoption agency and put together a scrapbook profiling our journey as a family with Tevin and Tyler for the agency to share with prospective birth mothers.

Within a few weeks, the agency contacted us about a mother six weeks away from delivery who wanted to place her baby girl with us. The whole process contrasted sharply with our experience getting the twins. We met the birth mother before Kenzie was born. We took her out to dinner and bought her a cell phone so that she could contact us when she went into labor. When she gave birth, we were both there in the delivery room. The doctor allowed me to cut the umbilical cord, then handed the swaddled infant to Paul, who marveled over her head of dark hair. He held her for the mother to see, and she smiled and kissed the baby's cheek—a goodbye kiss, a mark of profound love, a brave and generous blessing to her life with us, two men who knew nothing of motherhood, of childbirth, of the ultimate act of faith: to give life, and to give life again.

In that room, we cradled the baby, we cooed over her. We wept, mostly for joy, but also for the grief of separating a child from her mother, despite the mother's resolve to give her up. We thanked her the best we could. She shrugged and waved us away before the tears had a chance to pool in her eyes, before her heart could start to ache. But we were grateful, and we vowed to do the best we could—to give this child everything we had, to make the most of her precious life.

***

After Suzie stomped off and the girls were on stage performing the next number, the other mothers swarmed around me.

"We agree with you, Randy," one of them said while the others nodded emphatically to show their support. "There is absolutely no good reason why Mackenzie can't have you—or Paul, for that matter—backstage to help her get ready."

"They're all wearing bodysuits," another chimed in. "Nothing is exposed. No one should feel threatened."

"And making you go to a different room would be totally unfair to Mackenzie and to you," a third mother argued.

I accepted a few quick hugs and thanked them for coming to my defense.

After that day, at future competitions, Kenzie would cast sideways glances at me in the dressing room. She would forever remain on guard about my presence there. Soon she would hold out her arms for me to hand over her costumes and accessories. She would calmly assure me, "I can take care of it myself, Dad. You can go."

But that day, she was still my little girl—apprehensive and sadly aware now of the tensions life could present. Backstage, between acts, I zipped up her dress and teased out her hair. I wished her luck and kissed her cheek. I snapped photos. I watched her leap across the stage and scurry over to the wings, where I met her for a big hug.

When the event was over and the excitement died down, we found Daddy Paul and the three of us walked together to the parking lot. Paul helped us carry everything out. Kenzie grabbed my palm, and the smallness of her hand in mine surprised me. I tried to brace for what I knew was coming—the day she would become Lola; the day she would break my heart. I kissed her hand. For a little while longer, she needed me. For a little while longer, she would hold on.

8: High Anxiety

Paul

Three days before my scheduled surgery, I woke up and began my usual routine of taking out O'Neal, our Border Collie mix, and rousing the kids while Randy maintained his usual routine of snoozing. After feeding O'Neal and filling his water bowl, I made sure the kids were awake and started getting ready for work. My efficiency in taking care of the household on weekday mornings allowed Randy to slumber until the last possible minute, then shave and dress in a hurry and rush out the door. I didn't mind, unless his routine somehow collided with mine—for example, if his car was at the shop for repairs and I had to drive him to work. Invariably, this would add more time than necessary to the drive across town, since Randy's lateness meant missing the window for a smooth commute and hitting the worst part of rush-hour.

Fortunately, I didn't have to drive Randy to the hospital that day, but I felt the first signs of a different kind of setback as I pulled into the parking lot of Shelby Traditional Academy, where I worked as a counselor. I thought it was the beginning of a sinus infection. The bright mat of new grass on the school grounds reminded me it was allergy season. As I walked across the parking lot, I noted that the urban landscape of downtown Louisville was alive with pink and white blossoms and those unseen nuisances known as tree pollens. I blamed the trees for my headache and scratchy throat.

I put on a smile when I passed a few students and teachers on the way to my office. I was trying to remember whether I had any sinus medication in my desk drawer. I felt a twinge of remorse for delaying the prostatectomy, which Dr. Bell's office wanted me to undergo sometime in April. I had needed to wait until May because I was in charge of our school's state testing that took place in April. Student performance on the test was high stakes, with results determining our school's growth and funding. As the sole administrator at our site who was qualified for the role, I had to make sure faculty and staff adhered to the strict rules and regulations that governed the process. If I'd been able to schedule the prostatectomy in April before peak allergy season, however, I probably wouldn't have had to worry about developing a sinus infection three days before surgery.

In my office, I found some over-the-counter medication in my office and washed it down with water before settling at my desk to finish planning the school's annual Career Day. We had about thirty people coming to talk about their professions as chefs, firefighters, dog trainers, taekwondo instructors, and other occupations. Students got to pick three sessions they wanted to attend, and my job was organizing the schedule based on those preferences.

The headache and sore throat stayed with me as the morning hours dragged by. By lunchtime, I wanted to put my head on my desk and go to sleep. Although the sinus symptoms were typical for me this time of year, I couldn't imagine why I felt so lethargic. I knew I'd have to get checked out after school. I sent Randy a text message to let him know and to see whether he could pick up Kenzie and DeSean after school.

I left that afternoon at my usual time, after the buses departed. The sky was deep blue and the air felt a bit muggy, a typical Kentucky spring day. Bits of pollen were floating across the parking lot—another common sign of spring in our region—yet I wasn't sneezing. I stopped at the immediate care center on Taylorsville Road, a few miles from our neighborhood, and, after an hour-and-a-half-long wait, was called back to a room where a nurse took my vitals, announcing my blood pressure and body temperature were normal. She then showed me to an exam room, where I waited for another twenty minutes to see the doctor on duty. I told him my symptoms, and he checked my ears and used a small flashlight to look inside my mouth. "There's some inflammation, so we'll do a quick test for strep," he said, writing some notes on a clipboard and leaving the room.

The nurse reappeared a few minutes later and, while unwrapping a giant cotton swab, explained that she would be taking a sample from the back of my throat. "This might be a little uncomfortable for a second," she advised me. She motioned for me to tilt my head back and open my mouth. I closed my eyes to brace for the cotton tip stabbing my already tender throat tissue. I must have gagged reflexively.

"I'm sorry," she murmured, sounding sincere. She must have been used to this sort of reaction. "We'll get this tested and let you know something in a few minutes."

I sat alone in the exam room feeling despondent. I had talked to Randy on the phone on the way over, and he had warned me that the surgery would have to be delayed if I had an infection. I had been on edge for three months. I wanted to get it over with. Besides, the scheduling process had been a nightmare. I dreaded all the juggling and shuffling around that we would have to do to reschedule the surgery.

Ten minutes later, the doctor returned with a frown on his face. "The rapid test is positive. We'll do a culture and confirm the results. Meanwhile, we need to get you on an antibiotic and get this cleared up." He asked me the name of the pharmacy we used; they would call in the prescription.

"I'm supposed to have surgery in three days," I informed him, and anxiety washed over me, the realization hitting me again with new force: I had cancer. I was having an organ removed. I wondered whether the cancer had weakened my immunity.

"Well, that's probably going to be have to be postponed," he replied. "You'll need to call your surgeon's office and let them know."

I heaved a sigh and slid off the exam table. The doctor instructed me to rest, drink plenty of fluids, and gargle with warm salt water as needed to relieve my throat pain. I thanked him and left, feeling run down, physically and mentally.

Besides being stressed about having to reschedule my surgery, I also fretted about Randy's and my health insurance coverage and the financial burden of my treatment. It annoyed me to think about how much cheaper my medical costs would be if we were considered a married couple—if we had family coverage, rather than single-parent policies. We had to have separate health insurance policies not only for ourselves but for our children. I carried coverage on myself, the twins, and DeSean, while Randy held policies for himself and Kenzie. We paid higher premiums, double copays, and excessive out-of-pocket expenses for our family of six. It was ridiculous and unnecessary.

I headed directly home from the immediate care center; Randy had agreed via text message to return later for my prescription. The whole health insurance debacle got me thinking of all the other economic disadvantages we faced as a gay couple—such as our income tax-filing status and rights to each other's retirement benefits. They weren't new issues, but I pondered them anew, as though for the first time. Randy handled our finances, so these were typically his worries, but I was distressed about the situation and uneasy about our future.

I rubbed my eyes and concentrated on the pavement markings, the solid yellow lines and the broken ones. I remembered Randy's complaints about insurance premiums and taxes. We had to file our taxes separately and paid higher income taxes as a result, and if either of us died as the result of an injury at work, the survivor would not receive the worker's compensation benefit that married couples were entitled to. We also didn't qualify for death benefits paid to surviving spouses through Social Security or federal pensions. Even our auto insurance rates were negatively affected by the fact that we were a gay couple.

I tried to focus on the highway ahead of me and the fact that my destination was only a few minutes away, but my mind kept wandering to the list of things I had to do—the phone calls that needed to be made, the calendars that would have to be scrutinized to reschedule my surgery. I realized how fortunate our family had been, the fact that we had all been pretty healthy.

The toughest medical issue we had faced had been nine years earlier, when Tyler was diagnosed with proteinuria, a condition where the body either overproduces protein or the kidneys don't properly filter protein, resulting in protein in the urine. He'd had to undergo a kidney biopsy at eight years old. That had been the first time we realized that any health-related condition would be twice as taxing on our family since we not only had the illness itself to deal with, but also the possibility of prejudice based on the race of our children or my and Randy's sexual orientation.

There had been only one pediatric nephrology physician in town to consult regarding Tyler's disease, so our only other option would have been seeking treatment in Cincinnati or Indianapolis, a minimum two-hour drive one way. We had decided to try the local physician. We knew we would have to watch for the reactions of the physicians and office staff to our family dynamics. The process was like coming out all over again.

Thankfully, we hadn't encountered any difficulties at the doctor's office or at Kosair Children's Hospital, where the biopsy was performed. As Tyler's legal parent and the policyholder on his insurance, I'd been the one who had to sign the consent and other paperwork, which made Randy feel uninvolved and insignificant. However, while being prepped for surgery, Tyler had been comforted by Daddy Randy, who was a nurse, after all, and familiar with the machines and equipment; Randy had conversed easily with the hospital staff about their procedures and had winked at Tyler as though he had everything under control. Randy had always been affectionate with the twins, and in that moment I was grateful for that special blend of love and professionalism that made him so beautifully suited for the medical field.

The biopsy had been a painful procedure requiring general anesthesia and an overnight stay at the hospital. Tyler had been groggy for several hours afterward. The biopsy later revealed no sign of kidney disease, and soon after that, Tyler would begin taking medication to control the condition.

During his hospital stay, two of his teachers from the Brown School had visited with balloons and a stuffed animal. I had been moved by their kindness, and Tyler had managed a smile, despite his obvious discomfort. He hadn't smiled since Daddy Randy had blown up a surgical glove in pre-op.

"How do you feel?" one of the teachers, Ms. Shelly, had asked.

"Sore," was all Tyler had revealed, shifting under the sheets and frowning, as though testing to see whether the movement still hurt. He had moved very little all day, and that had concerned me. Now I knew why.

Randy had brought Tevin to visit that afternoon and later the two of them had gone home while I stayed the night at the hospital with Tyler. Someone on the staff had brought in a recliner for me, and I'd spent the evening working crossword puzzles, playing solitaire, and reading while Tyler rested. I remember time going by slowly and being able to sleep only intermittently that night—in those precious hours between rounds, after the nurses had checked Tyler's vitals. But it seemed as soon as I dozed off, someone shuffled into the room and the blood pressure machine coughed to life.

At some point I'd gotten up to use the bathroom. I remember gazing down at the small, sweet face in the darkened room and wondering why such a young, innocent child had to suffer this way. I had brushed my hand across his cheeks and forehead. I had prayed a silent prayer and made the sign of the cross over Tyler's sleeping body, the way my mother would have.

9: Critical Caring

Randy

The day of Paul's surgery felt like it would never come, and when the day finally arrived, it felt like it would never end. We got up extra early to be at the hospital by six AM. Both of us were groggy milling around between the bedroom and the bathroom, shaving, getting dressed. Paul was even more quiet than usual, which I took as a sign of nervousness. I gave him his space and checked in with Tevin and Tyler, who were getting ready for school.

"Don't forget to pick up Kenzie and DeSean today," I reminded Tevin.

He nodded.

"And I'll be driving straight from rehearsal to the hospital," Tyler confirmed.

"Good," I said, and I clapped him on the back.

The plan was for everyone to come to the hospital to see Dad after surgery. In truth, I didn't know whether the hospital would allow the kids to visit. Technically, only next of kin were permitted in recovery, which would exclude me and Kenzie, since legally she was my child only, not Paul's, and legally I was nothing more than a domestic partner to Paul. Regardless, we were hoping for the best, but we had explained to the kids, and they understood there could be difficulties.

When Paul was ready, we loaded up and headed out. The drive to Norton Hospital was oddly peaceful, and we merged onto the freeway into a small stream of vehicles heading west. It was still too early for gridlock. From the exit ramp leading us into the downtown area, every traffic light stayed on green, and we sailed straight through each one, reaching the hospital in record time. I wanted to think that was a sign of how our day would unfold—with no logjams or troublesome staff who might question our relationship and raise objections to my being there.

Once inside the hospital, we waited to be eyeballed suspiciously. This was the most tiresome part of being a gay couple—having to be on alert at all times. Paul and I had learned to approach potentially discriminatory situations this way, by feeling people out and watching their reactions.

We signed in at the registration desk. I lingered a short distance behind Paul and shoved my hands in my pockets, doing my best to fade into the background, which usually seemed the most effective way of handling the unknown. I couldn't help feeling self-conscious. I wondered what would happen if someone noticed, if the question was raised and we were forced to explain ourselves. Would they escort me to the door, leaving Paul to face one of the most difficult situations of his life alone? I felt angry and fearful. I could not, for the life of me, understand why we had to be treated this way, like disobedient children. It was wrong. It was insulting.

Paul got an armband and not long after that, he was called to pre-op, where a phlebotomist drew blood and a nurse started his IV. I stayed with him. I was relieved when Dr. Bell stopped by. He was as calm and confident as ever and spoke with us briefly about the surgery and aftercare.

While Paul was out of the room, I made it a point to thank Dr. Bell for agreeing to do the surgery. "I just want you to know that you're not only saving Paul's life, you're saving mine, too. I couldn't imagine my life without him, so I hope you'll do everything you can to make sure he gets the best care possible."

Dr. Bell nodded empathetically. "I understand your concern, and you have my word, Randy. We have an excellent team here, and of course I'll give Paul my very best."

I wanted to hug him but shook his hand instead. At least I knew Dr. Bell wouldn't run me out of the recovery room.

When the anesthetist showed up, I let him know of Paul's sensitivity to medication. I was remembering specifically the biopsies and other medical procedures he had undergone—for instance, the time he had fallen into a deep sleep after getting a mild analgesic.

"We'll take good care of him," the anesthetist assured me.

I stayed with Paul as long as possible, intently observing the way the staff looked at us, trying to figure out whether they saw us as being together, whether they assumed we were a couple. I expected someone to ask about our relationship. No one did.

I was relieved when my sister Violet, nephew Brian, and niece Nicki showed up. They were reliable allies and provided moral support in every family crisis we had. I rushed down to the lobby to meet them and showed them to pre-op holding, where Paul was awaiting sedation.

He sat up and smiled when we entered his curtained section of the bay. "Thank you all so much for coming by," he said.

Violet weaved her way to the head of the bed and rested her hand on Paul's head. "Don't you worry one bit, sweetheart. This will all be over with before you know it." She kissed his forehead.

Nicki followed suit, leaning over the bed to give Paul a kiss. "I love you, Uncle Paul," she said, rubbing his arm and backing away so that Brian could move forward.

"Good luck," Brian said, grasping Paul's hand and squeezing it in both of his, the way I had Dr. Bell's; it was a true show of affection. "I got to get on to work to take care of some computer software issues, but I wanted to let you know I'll be thinking of you and hoping for a speedy recovery."

He waved as he left. We all said goodbye.

Soon the nurse came in to start Paul's sedation. Violet and Nicki slipped out. I stayed behind and held Paul's hand until the surgical assistants came to roll him away. He gazed up at me with heavy eyes and smiled. I kissed his hand. "See you later," I said, and he nodded and relaxed against the pillow, the sedative working its magic. I stood watching as they wheeled him down the hallway.

The next few hours crawled by. Violet and Nicki kept me company. I called Paul's sister Katie, his brother Mike, and his father and promised to keep them updated. Then we walked to the cafeteria to get breakfast. I had been up for several hours by then and was famished. Afterward we returned to the waiting room, where a man next to us kept casting curious glances my way anytime I mentioned Paul's name. After noticing him, I was careful not to refer to Paul as my significant other. I didn't want to cause a scene or jeopardize my already precarious position.

I had learned the rule of silence from my mother, Frances. She had accepted my relationship with Paul, but felt that our vulnerability was simply the cost of being a gay couple in the same way she and her husband, Otis, had been viewed by some in the church as adulterers for remarrying.

"Let them think what they want," she told me once after I complained about the hateful looks some of the neighbors gave us when we lived at the house on Delk Road. "We're not perfect, and they're not either."

My siblings and I lost our mother too soon to heart disease and diabetes. The dye in the cardiac catheterization that was used to diagnose her heart condition had caused her kidneys to fail, and she spent the last five years of her life on dialysis. Otis drove her three times a week for treatment. She suffered miserably those last years and often cried out, "Jesus, take me home!" By the time of her last hospital visit, September 4, 2001, she was legally blind, and part of her right foot had been amputated due to gangrene.

That last time she was admitted, I had stopped by on my way home from work. My sister Myrtle was there, too. Mom was so heavy and weak that the orderly almost dropped her getting her into a wheelchair.

Now reclined in the hospital bed, Mom told us, "I've been seeing angels around me all day. John was here, too," she said, referring to our stepdad who had died twenty years ago in the train wreck in Belmont.

Myrtle shot me an alarmed look, but I didn't dismiss Mom's visions. I simply tried to console her and acknowledge her suffering. "You've been through a lot, Mom. It's been hard."

I felt guilty getting up to leave.

Mom sat up and patted the bed. "Come here, Randy."

I sat next to her and held her hand. Suddenly her grip on me tightened, the color draining from her face. Her mouth fell open and her glazed eyes widened, seemingly to some unseen terror.

"Mom, it's okay to let go," I whispered.

She clutched my hand. "Are you going to be okay, Randy?"

"Yes, Mom. I'll be fine."

She reached out and hugged me then, "I love you, son."

I knew she was trying to say goodbye. "I love you, too, Mom."

The next moment she was limp in my arms. She'd had a heart attack. I'd known all along.

Myrtle stood up and cried out, her body quivering, shoulders hunched, knees weak with grief.

A pair of orderlies rushed into the room to start compressions. I stopped them. "Let her go."

For the next few minutes, I stayed with her and thought of the pain leaving her body. I selfishly wondered how I could go on without her and questioned if I had lied to her by claiming I would be fine. I had called Violet, and I waited until she arrived with Otis and our brother Willie, and then I hurried out the door.

The tears started as I was leaving, and I wasn't sure they would ever stop. I got in my car trying to remember how to get home. I felt lost. Everything was a blur. The world had gone black. My mother had left us, but somehow I felt like the one who was missing—as though I had fallen into a darkness I might never come back from.

And then I remembered Paul and our boys, and I drove into the dusk toward my future. Toward my family.

***

By the time an assistant came out to let us know the surgery was over and that Paul was doing fine in the recovery room, it seemed days had passed. I reluctantly said goodbye to my sister and niece. Violet had been my rock since our mother died—Violet and Myrtle both. The two of them had taken over the worrying for Mom, always rushing to my side and sympathizing when Paul or the kids or I had any injustice to cope with.

I felt nervous approaching the recovery area. As a health care professional, I knew I was up against a system that had the legal right to discriminate against us. It didn't matter that Paul and I were soul mates, that we had committed our lives before God, or that we had raised a family together. Never mind that, as hokey as it sounded, I would have literally braved the shark-infested waters of the Florida straits for him or trudged alone across the sands of Death Valley to be with him—that's how powerful our love was.

And yet, none of that mattered. As much as we liked to claim we lived in the land of the free and the home of the brave, those platitudes didn't apply to Paul and me because we were a gay couple. And being gay, in America anyway, meant that we were less than; being gay supposedly was a choice we had made, so, therefore, we had to deal with the consequences.

But our love was not a choice—it was a fact. I had not come out as gay before meeting Paul. I had simply fallen in love with him. And that love was strong enough and real enough to help me conquer any fear of facing the truth about who I was. In reality, the only choice Paul and I ever made was to tell the truth about who we were and to try to live authentically.

The recovery room was a clean, spacious area lined with beds and filled with the quiet hum of machinery and monitoring devices. It was a familiar sight to me, having spent many years as a recovery room nurse, yet I panicked when I saw Paul lying there, looking frail and pale. Any fear I had of being an illegal visitor was replaced by what now felt like an instinct to respond.

A nurse was with him. I moved in close on the opposite side of the bed and brushed his arm. "How do you feel?"

He closed his eyes and grimaced in pain. "I hurt," he mumbled. "I hurt bad."

I turned to the nurse. "Any significant pain whatsoever is unacceptable."

Her dark eyes flashed at me.

"You need to titrate the medication to meet his needs."

She spun around and promptly administered a dose of morphine.

I saw the bag from Paul's catheter hanging off the side of the bed's metal frame. It was filled with bloody fluid. I made a mental note to keep the kids from that side of the bed.

Paul was resting. The medication had kicked in. This was a good time, I told myself. It had to be now. I tried not to think about what I was doing. Without hesitating, I returned to the waiting area and quietly escorted the kids into the recovery room. Tevin and Tyler lingered at the foot of the bed. I stood with Kenzie and DeSean at Paul's side until his eyes fluttered open. Kenzie made a sad face. Paul forced a smile. We all giggled softly. Paul drifted back to sleep.

Afterward we stayed in the waiting area while the staff moved him to a post-operative room, then we all huddled into the elevator to ride up to transitional care.

Kenzie wanted to press the button. DeSean waved his hands, magician-like, over the control panel, as though he might punch another number just for fun. The twins laughed. At seventeen, Tevin and Tyler were as tall as me, yet I still worried over them as though they were children. Being at the hospital together always reminded me of their birth, and the moment Paul and I had become parents, and how we had held them in our arms and wept. There was a nurse at the Paducah hospital who had taken offense when she learned that Paul and I would be fostering the twins. I remembered her glaring at us, the hate in her eyes, as though we were criminals, as though we were evil. Paul and I had looked at each other. Our joy had turned to dread. But soon the other nurses and medical assistants had noticed her reaction, and they had steered her away from us.

And here we stood, seventeen years later, still a family. I wondered whether we were still vulnerable. I wondered whether we would ever see an end to all the hate.

We spilled out of the elevator into transitional care and made our way to Daddy Paul's room, all of us smiling, determined to raise his spirits, determined to help him heal. As heads began to turn our way, I said a silent prayer. I held Kenzie's hand.

As it turned out, the nursing staff didn't flinch at our family constellation. It was as if they had known us all our lives. It was as if they had been expecting us.

10: The Healing

Paul

After surgery, I felt old for the first time in my life. At first, it was the excruciating pressure and burning of the catheter that crippled me. The slightest tug on the rubber tubing that ran through my urethra felt like the violent yank of a practiced fisherman attempting to disembowel me while reeling me in. Then it was the pain of the prostatectomy radiating from my groin to my abdomen. I had a low threshold for pain to begin with, so what was mild discomfort for most patients was moderate discomfort for me.

By the time I returned home the next day, my muscles and joints were stiff from being immobile, and over the next few days, the aches and pains that go along with lying around grew worse.

A week later—much to Randy's chagrin—I followed through with plans to return to work temporarily. I was on the school committee to select a new principal, and we were interviewing candidates for the position.

One of my colleagues greeted me when I arrived and showed me into the conference room so that I could get comfortable. The committee chair thanked me for coming in and asked how my recovery was going.

"I'm still pretty sore, but to be honest, I'm just happy to get out of the house for a few hours and focus on something else," I said and started scanning through the packet of material in preparation for the interviews.

The biggest issue was the catheter and urinary drainage bag I had strapped to my leg, which was concealed by my clothes but still made me feel self-conscious. I didn't mention this to my coworkers, who graciously avoided scrutinizing me, as though sensing my unease. They were quick to offer help when I made any motion to get up, and after the interviews, everyone wished me well and made me promise to let them know if I needed anything. This is the blessing of working in public education. The people are genuinely caring; the profession demands it.

Just when I'd gotten used to draining the bag, and getting dressed each morning and moving around without pulling on the tubing, it was time to have the catheter removed. Randy accompanied me to my post-op checkup two weeks after surgery. He waited outside while the nurse removed the catheter, a process that was not only embarrassing, but also unbearably painful. At one point, I thought I might faint. It felt as though she were ripping my guts out. When it was over, I made no objection to the nurse's orders to take it easy for the rest of the day and let Randy take care of things.

At home, I was afraid to urinate on my own, anticipating a sensation not unlike that of the catheter coming out. I stood at the toilet for several minutes waiting for the urine to flow, or, rather, waiting for my mind to let it flow. I breathed a sigh of relief when it came, a slow trickle, burning a bit at first, then streaming steadily, like a river of worry leaving my body.

Although that marked the toughest hurdle of my recovery, I had to limit my activity for the next four weeks, which meant no running or rigorous exercise. Since I had to retrain my body to control my bladder with only one urethral sphincter—the second sphincter muscle is located within the prostate and, thus, was removed with the gland—I experienced incontinence for several weeks. Walking into the drugstore to purchase a box of Depends was probably the biggest factor that made me feel rundown and old. Naturally, this affected my mood. Randy assured me it was temporary, but I knew I would not feel one hundred percent better until I could resume my normal physical routine, as well as regain control of my bladder.

One night during dinner, Randy suggested writing a letter to the CEO of Norton Hospital commending the staff for the excellent customer care our family had received there.

"You know, Dad, we've been talking about doing this," Randy said, his blue-green eyes gleaming. "It was such a great experience for a change. Our relationship was made known to the staff. We were treated like a regular couple. Our family was treated like a regular family. I had no problem getting in to see you before or after the surgery. The kids were there. No awkward moments." He threw open his hands.

All I could do was nod in agreement. He was right. He seemed intent on writing the letter. Besides, I thought, maybe it would get my mind off the negatives—the incontinence and lack of exercise doing me in. "Yes, I think we should."

"Good! Let's knock it out tonight." Randy held me in his gaze, waiting for a response.

"Okay," I said, perhaps not as enthusiastically as he would have hoped.

I later followed Randy into the home office, where we settled at the computer to compose the letter.

Randy did an Internet search to find the hospital's CEO and contact information. "Okay. Steve Williams." He worked quickly and efficiently, formatting the document and typing the name and address. Next, he ticked off a list of compliments he wanted to include, glancing at me for approval, and outlined them on the page.

"I think it's important to point out the fact that they focused on holistic care, which is really critical to the patient's experience and recovery. The nurse and the staff—they all knew you had a partner and kids, and they respected that. They understood that your spiritual health and psychological well-being directly affects your physical health." He was typing as he talked.

I propped an elbow on the desk and rested my head on my hand, admiring his command over the keyboard.

He read the kudos aloud and looked at me sharply, holding his chin. "Which of those do you think is the most important?"

Although I didn't bring much energy to the task, I was glad for the time together and the opportunity to look back on all the good in what could have been an even more harrowing situation. It felt like making a gratitude list with the love of my life at the very top. Watching him work, I was reminded of everything I loved about him—his drive and determination, his way with words. He paused for a moment, and I whisper laughed at his charm and compassion.

"What?" he wanted to know, a playfully alarmed expression on his freckled face.

I bowed my head, a bit embarrassed, trying hard to find a way to articulate how I felt. "You're sweet, Dad. I love you." I rubbed one of the hands he had poised over the keyboard, which was as soft as the day we met, as soft as the heart of this man. I kissed him, quickly, shyly, and he grinned and giggled like a little boy.

"I love you, too, Dad," he said, sitting up straighter, his shoulders expanding, his smile broadening like a giant sun lighting up the world.

11: New Lease on Life

Randy

I was slower and more sluggish than usual waking up at the Embassy Suites in Nashville, which was typical whenever I was on a business trip. I tapped my cell phone snooze button several times before rolling out of bed. By then, I only had an hour before the planning meeting started, and I was supposed to join a couple of my colleagues for breakfast first. After a quick shower, I toweled off and was rounding up my clothes when my phone rang. I was expecting a call from Paul, but not so soon. He'd had his blood work done at Dr. Bell's office and was waiting to hear the results.

"Good morning," I answered.

When Paul echoed back, "Good morning," I was relieved.

"Well, is it a good morning?" I wanted to know.

"Yes," Paul said. "It's a very good morning."

My heart leapt in my chest. "The blood work came back?"

"It did."

I was most interested in Paul's prostate-specific antigen test, which measures the amount of PSA in the blood. The lower the PSA, the better. Higher amounts would have indicated the cancer remained. At the time of his diagnosis, Paul's PSA was nineteen, which was moderately high. Anything below ten is considered normal or low risk.

"Good news on your PSA?"

"Yes. Really good news. It was zero."

"Zero? Are you kidding me? That's incredible!" I punched the air, victory style.

"It's as close to a clean bill of health as you can get after prostate surgery." Paul's voice was lighter than it had been in months. "I still have to go back for checkups every few months or so, but, yeah, I'm really happy."

"We'll have to celebrate when I get back," I said, suddenly remembering my meeting. "Hey, I've got to get dressed and head down to breakfast. Can I call you later?"

"Sure. I didn't mean to keep you. I just wanted to let you know about the test results."

"I'm so glad you did. It just made my day. Love you."

"Love you, too."

I slipped into pants and shirt, grateful to be dressing business casual for a change, then combed my hair and went down to breakfast. I found Bill and Kevin at a table in the corner and greeted them with a wide grin.

Bill was a few years older than I was, with gray speckled hair and deep wrinkles. His face was always a bit puckered, his lips drawn tightly together, and he had a tendency to look people up and down when they were in full view. He did this to me when I approached. I ignored him as I pulled out a chair and sat down.

"What are you smiling about?" Kevin finally asked.

I considered my approach. Here were a couple of coworkers—Bill, in fact, was my boss—who did not yet know that I was gay. I tried to be cautious about revealing this fact in the workplace, limiting it to only the most relevant circumstances. In fact, when I first started working as a manager at the hospital in 1998, I had revealed nothing about my partner or my family for the first three months. I had stayed out of conversations about family and personal affairs. I had made nothing known because I wanted the people I worked with to get to know me before making a judgment about my sexual orientation and my unconventional family. After three months on the job, I'd taken out my photos of Tevin and Tyler and put them on my desk. I had started talking about Paul and the kids when appropriate, and not one of my coworkers had expressed any sort of hostility or disdain toward me.

Over the last twenty years, I had learned strategies over the last twenty years to protect my partner and, later, our children from discrimination, like referring to Paul in generic terms, like "other half." I had hoped to quietly persuade those with bias to accept us as a regular family with the same dreams and desires as other families. At the same time, our personal quest for stability, success, and happiness had meant making some tough decisions in our early years together—for example, the decision to move from Bullitt County to Old Louisville, precipitated by our need to raise the twins in a more diverse community.

***

It was 1996. We had celebrated Tevin and Tyler's first birthday at the house on Delk Road in February, and President Bill Clinton, who in his first term had instituted a new policy on gays in the military known as "Don't Ask, Don't Tell," was running for reelection against Bob Dole and Ross Perot. That spring, the Supreme Court had ruled against a constitutional amendment in Colorado that kept cities, towns, and counties from seeking legal action to protect the rights of homosexuals in *Romer v. Evans*. Although the wheels of justice were beginning to turn in favor of gay rights, and the boys were still too young to comprehend racism, life in rural Kentucky was proving to be increasingly difficult for Paul and me.

No one we knew would dare say an unkind word around the boys, but we lived in the shadows of a bigoted community where racial slurs were common and anti-gay sentiment was strong. I hadn't planned to move away from my mom and family, but Paul and I realized that raising two black kids in a place where there were no other black people and where people habitually used the "N" word would be cruel and unfair to Tevin and Tyler, not to mention grueling for us.

Even before the boys were born, we had both experienced conflict about living in Belmont in the early 1990s, the era of literal "gay bashing," when people were being brutally beaten and murdered because of their sexual orientation.

Paul and I were afraid to leave the house, especially after dark. He drove seven miles every day to run the track at Bullitt Central High School in Shepherdsville because he was terrified to run on the barren country roads around our neighborhood. My family was well liked, yet we were fearful of our neighbors.

Paul had earned some respect shooting hoops at the end of our driveway with the teenagers who lived next door, but the physical threats always loomed. When one of us mowed the lawn around Mom's property, we were constantly vigilant of what was going on around us. We were paranoid that we might not hear someone sneak up on us over the roar of the mower's engine. There was one neighbor in particular who would watch us cutting the grass. He was a tall, thin young man, with shaggy blond hair, and sometimes he would stand shirtless staring out at us across his muddy patch of yard until the telephone inside his house beckoned or the mower sputtered to a stop. He and his friends would crank up AC/DC while they drank beer and worked on their cars. When they spotted us outside, they would mutter something indistinct and laugh.

The preacher from Belmont Baptist Church was one of our neighbors. He was no different from the others. When he retired, Mom had deeded off a half acre to him, and he had moved his daughter's trailer onto it. He and his wife, his daughter, and at least one grandson lived there. This happened while I was away at college; since Mom and my stepdad, Otis, thought so highly of the preacher, I couldn't say much about it, but I eventually came to resent his proximity to us.

The preacher was probably one of the biggest reasons we decided to move. Neither Paul nor I could shake the memory of the summer day in 1992 when he came over to warn us about a suspicious person in the area. Mom was babysitting for some friends, and Otis, Paul, and I were sitting on the porch talking about nothing and everything that came to mind. Brother O'Dell strolled over wearing a polyester shirt and denim pants. His coppery colored hair was cut short in a fade, and he wore gold wire-rim glasses that he fussed with all the time, pushing them up the bridge of his wide nose, taking them off and cleaning the lenses with a white handkerchief that he kept in his back right pocket.

He waddled up the porch steps onto the deck, all the while squinting against the sun. After Otis greeted him, he got right down to business. "I got to tell ya 'bout something, and you better listen up," he said with a sneer. His tone was serious, as though he was delivering a sermon. "A nigger was seen down on the railroad tracks earlier today."

Although I wasn't surprised by his language, I had grown more sensitive to the preacher's bigotry since returning from Berea College, and a flush of anger came over me. I looked at Paul, who was gaping up at O'Dell, wide-eyed. I had warned him of the preacher's antics. Now he was witnessing it for himself.

He spoke primarily to Otis, whose face was stoic, his eyes focused on the preacher. "Now, Otis, you all need to make sure you get all your valuables put away when you go in. Keep your doors locked. A nigger like that will come in and rob you blind," he said, making a sweeping gesture with his hand.

Paul kept staring at him, and I kept feeling more and more uncomfortable with the situation. When he finally toddled down the steps and back across the yard, Paul let out an audible sigh. He made no attempt to veil his feelings even with Otis sitting nearby. "Where did he come from? The Fifties?"

I shook my head and got up. "I need something to wash that taste out of my mouth. Do you need anything?"

"I'll go with you," Paul said. "I feel the urge to hide, but not from the man on the railroad tracks—from him!" He pointed to the blue and white trailer.

It was the memory of that incident that burned hottest in our minds when we decided to start looking for a house in the city. Telling my mother that warm spring day in 1996 was hard. The babies were inside with Paul, and Mom and I were sitting on the porch steps.

"We need a more open-minded community to raise the boys in," I explained, "a place where they'll come in contact with other blacks, where they won't feel so out of place."

Mom was visibly upset. Her mouth was set in a frown, the wrinkles deep around the corners of her mouth. "Those babies will never feel out of place around me, I promise you that!" Her voice choked, and her eyes grew watery.

I hugged her shoulders. "Oh, Mom. I know that. It's just so hard for us here, but not because of you or Otis. You all have been really good to us, and we appreciate that."

I let her sulk in silence for a few minutes, and then I started telling her about our plans and how she could be a part of them. "We want to get a fixer-upper. We thought maybe while we're working on it, you could help watch the twins."

She nodded quietly and kissed my cheek. "You know I'd do anything for you and Paul and those babies." And she drew up her chest, pulled herself up by the railing, and marched inside the house.

***

Sitting at the table that morning at the hotel with my boss and colleague, I remembered the new life Paul and I had found in the city, where we began to meet other gay and lesbian couples, and people of other races and ethnicities. Though life in Old Louisville had proven easier and more diverse than Bullitt County, we would soon come to understand that we had not completely escaped the bigotry.

For example, fast forward sixteen years, and here I was now, somehow intuitively aware that the news I was about to share would not sit well with my coworkers. Bill and Kevin watched me expectantly. Perhaps they knew. My heart screamed not to tell them, but my head said quite calmly, "You do not need their approval. Stop hiding."

So I told them. "I just talked to my partner, Paul, on the phone." I didn't bother gauging their reaction. I pretended to adjust my napkin on my lap. "He had prostate surgery three months ago," I said matter-of-factly. "This morning he found out that his PSA level is zero, which means no cancer." I looked up then and smiled.

Kevin's eyes darted uneasily from the plates on the table to the carpeted floor to the cheap dining room décor—framed watercolor prints, mirror tiles, and vases with dried flowers.

Bill's face puckered more tightly than normal, contorting as though he had been gut punched. He suddenly changed the subject. "So the meeting today is on—is on, um—is on—is on decreasing costs," he stammered. "We'll be looking at—um—partnering with other hospitals to improve efficiency."

I sagged in my seat. I had suspected that they didn't know I was gay, yet I had not been prepared for such a cold response. Essentially, I had just told them that my partner—who was the equivalent of my spouse—was no longer in peril, and essentially, they had told me with their callousness that the life of a gay man, or a gay couple, meant nothing to them—was actually gross and disturbing.

I wanted to slam my fists down on the table and rattle the silverware. I wanted to stand up and toss the table onto its side, sending plates and glasses and that crappy plastic centerpiece careening through the air. *Who are you to judge me?* I wanted to shout. *What makes your love for a woman any different or any better than my love for a man?*

I thought this was the worst it could get, but it was only the beginning. After that two-day strategy meeting in Nashville, Bill would attempt to sabotage my career, reassigning me to roles that put me farther and farther away from him—roles that belittled my abilities and threatened my future with the hospital.

For now, I was too mortified to speak, too paralyzed by shock to make any movement to rectify the situation. I simply sat slumped in my seat, all the joy of Paul's phone call drained out of me. I wished I could've left at that moment. I wished I could've gone home right then.

12: A Life and Death Lesson

Paul

Τhe school day was nearly over when Randy called. I was on bus duty waiting for the bell to ring.

"What's up?"

"It's O'Neal. He's in bad shape. DeSean's really upset. He was crying. He said O'Neal's sprawled out on the bedroom floor, and he hasn't moved since he got home from school."

"Oh no." I was standing in the hallway and had to duck back into my office to sit down. O'Neal was the border collie mix we had adopted from the Kentucky Humane Society when the twins were seven years old. Rescuing a dog had been my idea, but Randy had resisted until Tevin intervened with his clear-eyed second-grader's logic. "But you adopted us. Why can't we adopt this dog and give him a home like you did for us?" he had asked, his head tilted curiously, deep brown eyes fixed on Daddy Randy's face. The question had been impossible to answer without coming across as an unfeeling killjoy, and so Randy had relented, and we had picked up O'Neal the following day. It hadn't taken long for the twins and me to warm up to the dog, or for Randy to start complaining about the time we spent vacuuming the hairs shed from his long mottled coat.

"He should stay outside," Randy had argued in those first months.

"That's no way to treat a dog—throw him out in the back yard all by himself?" I had countered. Randy had been raised in a household where animals were kept outdoors, but I felt strongly that pets should be part of the family and should stay with the family.

Although Randy had a hard time adjusting to having a dog in the household, in the ten years we owned O'Neal, he had grown to love and accept him, if for nothing else than the sheer joy he gave me and the kids. O'Neal had bonded with me early on and started sleeping on the floor next to my side of the bed. For a while, I would wake up and nearly step on him getting out of bed. Gradually, though, I got into the habit of sliding down the mattress to the footboard, and O'Neal would pitter-patter in my wake, so I would take him outside to pee first thing. Afterward I fed him as an incentive to come back inside. It was a good routine. He became my dog, fiercely loyal to me in that sweet way of abandoned mutts. Randy sometimes feigned fighting with me to be entertained by O'Neal, who would bare his teeth and growl at him as though he were an intruder. He must have done so playfully, however; he had never snapped or lunged at Randy.

On the phone that day, I could tell that Randy was distressed because his voice trembled and he talked hurriedly. "I just called the vet and got an appointment for us to take him in at five-thirty. I'm on my way home now. You'll have to drive straight home for us to make it."

"I should be there by five," I told him and said goodbye, tucking away my phone. A dull ache started in my head, and I squeezed my eyes shut to ward off the pain. I had known this day was coming, yet I suddenly felt crushed by the weight of losing our furry friend. I grabbed my keys from my desk, shoved them in my pocket, and strode toward the bus-rider exit doors.

When the last run left the parking lot, I rushed to my truck and prayed that traffic would be light going home.

I recalled O'Neal's rapid decline over the past few weeks. I'd been having to coax him to eat and drink. He had lost control of his bowel movements lately and would relieve himself in the most unexpected places right out in the open, nowhere near a doorway, which would have shown he'd been making an effort to get outside. Despite the severity of these changes, I passed off all his symptoms as signs of aging, not of dying. After all, O'Neal was twelve years old now, a senior citizen. Driving home, I worried that I had been too selfishly attached to O'Neal to accept the seriousness of his condition. Just that weekend, we had hosted a potluck party for Randy's office, and one of his coworkers had jutted her lower lip at the sight of O'Neal lying so lifeless on the dining room floor. "You all need to have him put down."

At the time, I had been offended by her remark. I thought people in general too easily wrote off their sick pets and had them euthanized for the sake of convenience. Now I wondered whether I was responsible for prolonging O'Neal's suffering.

When I got to the house, Randy, DeSean, Kenzie, and Tevin were waiting, silent and sullen, in the bedroom.

"His breathing has slowed a lot," Randy said. "Can you help carry him to the truck?"

We put him in the back seat of the Explorer, and I climbed in next to him and stroked his coat, which looked matted and felt strangely stiff. Randy drove. Tevin rode in front. Kenzie sat mute in the middle seat with DeSean, who hung over the back so that he could hold O'Neal's paw on the drive to the vet's office. Springhurst was only twenty minutes away, but it seemed like an eternity. O'Neal's breathing was labored. It was painful to watch.

When we got there, the staff waved us through the waiting room directly into the back, where Randy and I carefully lowered the dog to the floor on the lion print blanket we'd used to carry him out of the house. It was an old blanket Randy had had in college. O'Neal was barely breathing now, his mouth slightly open, his long tongue dangling out, white and pasty. I rested a hand on his side and my fingers found the grooves of his ribs. He seemed smaller on that blanket on the floor of the vet's office. He seemed to have lost so much weight so quickly, shrinking and shriveling in a sad prelude to disappearing entirely from our lives. He had been a healthy, active dog, chasing the kids around the yard and sometimes getting loose and running after vehicles, particularly the UPS truck. He had an intense herding instinct and often paced the fence line in the back yard, wearing a dirt path into the lawn. Inside the house, he got so anxious watching cars pass that he had chewed up the windowsill in the dining room. My heart ached seeing his poor old body withered away.

The doctor stooped down to examine him. She checked his eyes, listened to his breathing, and turned to us. "I'm sorry, folks. He's dying, and there's not a whole lot that can be done for him at this point, other than end it more quickly to spare him any more pain."

Randy looked to me. I nodded without hesitation.

DeSean, Kenzie, and Tevin gathered around, each of them gently petting the dog's back and forming a circle around him. They were saying goodbye. I looked at my phone to check the time. We had called for Tyler, who was in rehearsal for the musical "Wiley and the Hairy Man," produced by StageOne Family Theatre. It was Tyler's first lead role. He had been cast as Wiley, a young boy whose best friend is a dog.

Tyler burst through the door just as the doctor was administering the injection. Perhaps playing that part in the musical made him sensitive to the situation, or maybe he was simply stunned by O'Neal's sudden demise, but as he scanned the room, I could see the emotion welling up, his eyes glazing with tears, his lips quivering. He dropped to the floor with a low moan, and Randy moved in to comfort him. I thought my heart would break from the sadness filling that room. We were all sniffling, but while Tyler was sobbing for the loss of O'Neal, the rest of us were weeping with relief. We had seen the dog's final hours; we had watched him struggle. Tyler had only witnessed the final dramatic scene, when the life left his body—what little life had remained.

I worried about Tyler—not just because of this outpouring of emotion for O'Neal, but the fact that he had always so openly expressed his feelings. The world was cruel to boys who wore their heart on their sleeve. And not only was Tyler expressive, but he had a gentle and happy disposition, was talkative, and as he grew, he became keenly interested in the performing arts. At age four, he took up dance at Patti Medley's Dance Center and thrived for six years there, focusing on tap, jazz, and ballet. At the age of eight, he auditioned for a TV commercial for The Crusade for Children and was among twelve kids selected to sing in the advertisement. In fifth grade, however, he ended up quitting dance class, overwhelmed by the taunting and teasing he suffered at school. Two years later, his interest in dance resurged, and we signed up three of our kids—Tyler, Tevin, and Kenzie—for classes at Dancensation Studios, where focus was placed not only on dance, but stage performance, including singing and acting.

As an arts lover, I was thrilled to see our children involved in song and dance. I had watched Tyler progress from a lively, energetic boy to an accomplished young actor and performer. Yet I feared for him now as a young black man in a culture that expected masculinity. I feared for his safety, and I fretted over the way others might treat him, and how that might destroy his self-confidence. I wished that I could protect Tyler somehow—cast a protective enchantment around him and all the kids the way Hermione does in *Harry Potter and the Deathly Hallows*. Although I had survived the cancer, I knew that I would not always be there for them, that I could not safeguard them against the dangers and the difficulties of the world.

Yet seeing them in that room at the vet's office gave me hope in their ability to cope with whatever came their way. In that moment of grief, my children lifted me up with the compassion and strength that they showed. They were brave. They were loving. They were kind. They were good. They were living proof of a higher love—a love that transcended gender, race, sexual identity, our ideas about family, and everything we believed love itself to be.

***

We left O'Neal's body at the vet's office to be cremated, and we drove home in silence. I slept hard that night, emotionally exhausted, and dreamed of lost children and a wailing siren that became the howl of a dog.

When I awoke the next morning at quarter 'til six, I rolled over, slipped to the bottom of the bed, and got up. It wasn't until I reached the kitchen that I realized the clicking paws hadn't followed me out the bedroom door. I stared down at O'Neal's water bowl. I tried to recall when it had ended, when exactly he had lost his spunk, his spirit. I remembered how the roar of trucks had once had him sprinting across the yard. The dark mornings I let him out on the lawn. The way he came to me whenever I called. How I bent over to thank him. The warmth of his fur in my hands. The soft body.

13: A Heart Unlocked

Paul

One Saturday in February, Randy and I were getting ready to go to a U of L basketball game when we started talking about having a party for Tevin and Tyler, who would be graduating from high school in the spring.

"When's Tevin's graduation again?" Randy asked while putting on his Cardinals polo shirt.

I pulled out my phone and checked the calendar. "May 19," I replied. "And Tyler's is June 6."

Their ceremonies would fall on different days since they went to different schools. Tevin attended Trinity, an all-male, college-preparatory Catholic high school, while Tyler was majoring in the performing arts at duPont Manual.

Randy suggested a party date sometime in June.

"Maybe I should invite my dad to come down for Tevin's graduation." Although my father and I had never been close, it would be a proud occasion for our boys, and I wanted their grandfather to be able to share in it.

I could see the disappointment in Randy's face. "But what about Tyler?"

"He won't be able to travel back down here for another ceremony that soon," I reasoned. My father was in his eighties, and traveling was difficult for him. Not only that, but two of my nephews would also be graduating that spring in New York, and I knew he would want to be in Jamestown for those occasions.

I shrugged. "I just figured Trinity is a Catholic school. They'll have a faith-based service. He would probably like that."

"You're exactly right," Randy said decidedly. "That's a great idea." He grabbed his jacket and his keys off the bed. "Are you ready to go?"

I gawked at him and threw open my arms to show him I was dressed. "I'm always ready before you are."

He laughed. "Just making sure."

***

I called my father that weekend to let him know Tevin's graduation date. "The ceremony is at Bellarmine University," I told him. "There's a baccalaureate mass the night before in Steinhauser Gym on the high school's campus."

Dad must have been contemplating. I knew he had heard me, but he was quiet on the other end of the line.

"You can stay with us," I offered, trying to make his decision easier. "We'll take you to the graduation events, and we'll make sure you have a ride to and from the airport."

I waited for his response. I hoped he would come—not for my sake, but for Tevin and Tyler's. I wanted to tell him this, but I didn't want to hurt his feelings. Our relationship had been strained over the years. There were things we would never agree on, a bitter cloud that hung between us no matter how much we tried to clear the air.

***

We had been at our best perhaps when I was eleven or twelve years old, during the 1970s, the golden years of the St. Bonaventure men's basketball team. For a couple seasons, Dad and I would make the hour-and-a-half drive from Jamestown to St. Bonaventure to see the games. He was a St. Bonaventure alumnus and must have gotten free tickets. The seats at Reilly Center were never good, always at the top of the bleachers, but the games were as exciting as the ones we watched on TV. The Brown Indians (later known as the Bonnies) had garnered a huge following after going to the NCAA Final Four in 1970, when Bob Lanier was on the team. Lanier had been drafted by the NBA and was playing for the Detroit Pistons in those days.

Sports were a big part of the Catholic tradition. We had catechism on Wednesday nights, church on Sundays, and some kind of sports practice or games to play in between. For me and my brothers, our involvement in sports began in fourth grade with the Northside Warriors youth football team. From August through November, we came home from school, put on our pads, and marched to Roseland Park for practice. This went on until eighth grade. I also played youth basketball at the YMCA. Later I would run track and follow in my brother Jim's' footsteps and play quarterback as a ninth grader at Washington Junior High School.

My parents came to all the games. For parents, the games were a social event, an extension of church. Mom and Dad cheered us on dutifully, collectively, but they never singled us out for individual praise. We were expected to do well, and to enjoy the game, and we did. There was no coaching from the sidelines or arguing with game officials. My father had been a basketball and football coach when he was still a high school English teacher. By the time I was born, he was working as a negotiator with the union, New York State United Teachers.

Even at the Brown Indians' basketball games that we attended together in my youth, my father remained fairly passive, clapping and grinning from his seat when the team made one of its stunning plays. However, he never forbid me from leaping up and waving my arms, whether it was in response to a player scoring points or simply a way for me to participate in halftime show antics along with the rest of the crowd.

I remember one particular December day when Dad and I left Jamestown in his Delta 88 heading east on one of the two-lane highways that would take us to St. Bonaventure. A few inches of snow had already accumulated on the roadways and more was falling. The radio was tuned to some AM station that played the kind of slow music we used to hear on the Lawrence Welk Show. My father watched the road intently, his gaze shifting to the rearview and side view mirrors, his hands evenly spaced on the steering wheel, his grip firm yet not tense the way I imagined my own hands would be had I been the one driving, but more like the hands of a lover leading a dance partner in a waltz. It was as though my father had an operating manual for his life, and he was the type of man who went by the book. Whatever he did, he did it well. He was not nervous that day but focused, and sitting next to him, I was keenly aware of his competence as we moved through that white landscape.

When we arrived at St. Bonaventure, the campus seemed quiet and peaceful, and as we walked to the Reilly Center, I wondered whether the game had been canceled because of the snow. But as we swung through the doors, the noise of the crowd and the smell of concession stand food hit me all at once. Dad got us hot dogs and sodas, and as we tramped our way to the bleachers, I took in the sights and sounds of the stadium: cheerleaders performing crazy stunts, college students with painted faces clutching posters and chanting rallying cries, massive banners strewn along the walls announcing titles and championships the team had won. There was much fervor surrounding the team. That was the year the Brown Indians would end up winning the National Invitational Tournament.

I remember watching the game and feeling the electricity in the air as the home team took control of the floor. I was in awe of the players, who glided easily across the court, the ball seemingly following in their wake, gravitating to the men in brown as though they were magnets. I could not contain my excitement when one of the mighty players sprang from the floor and executed a dunk so powerful I could hear the ball swooshing through the net from my seat in the nosebleed section. I wanted to see an instant replay of every spectacular move, and it was then that I began to appreciate the value of every moment of live, untelevised sports.

By the end of the night I was exhausted, and I dozed off on the ride home, dreaming I was flying over the court with a basketball filled with helium, the roar of the crowd ringing in my ears.

***

My father flew in from Jamestown for Tevin's graduation in mid-May. We welcomed him into our home and put him up in the master bedroom, since it was on the main floor and easiest to access. He greeted us with hugs and was genuinely surprised by how much the kids had grown. We had been in touch over the past year because of my prostate cancer, but I hadn't seen my father in over a year. He moved more slowly, I noticed, and seemed smaller in stature—this man who had always loomed over me, a giant in so many ways.

On Saturday, Randy and I took Dad to baccalaureate mass, where he seemed to be in his element. The procession included the archbishop, several priests, as well as Trinity's faculty and the graduating class, all in full regalia. There was a band and an all-male chorus, and the music mollified us while the 400 graduates filed in, Tevin among them, looking dapper but solemn from our vantage point in the Trinity gymnasium. My father nodded when I pointed Tevin out to him, his eyes smiling behind the large lenses of his light-rimmed glasses.

When all the graduates were finally seated, the priest gave a homily. Afterward we read scripture, prayed, and sang hymns. Dad seemed engaged in the service, particularly toward the end when communion was offered. The priest recited the Eucharistic Prayer while a dozen or so clergy set up stations around the auditorium to offer communion to students and audience members. Because the seating arrangements and my father's physical condition would have made it difficult for him to approach the station nearest us, I called one of the clergy over.

Dad nimbly reached into a chalice for a wafer, popped it into his mouth, and then accepted a sip of wine from a second chalice. The body and the blood of Christ. Randy and I did not partake because neither of us felt moved. I was no longer involved in the Catholic Church and had distanced myself from its organized rituals. I remembered when communion was important to me, my ticket to heaven, but I realized that excluding people from communion the way the Catholic Church had was not Christ-like.

When the service was over, Tevin met us in the parking lot, where we took turns snapping photos together before disbursing and heading home.

Later that evening when we were alone together, Randy suggested that my father might be opening up to our relationship.

"I doubt that," I countered.

"How do you know? He seems fine around us."

"I just know how he is. Believe me, his mind hasn't changed." I knew that Dad's devotion to the Catholic faith would not have allowed him to fully embrace our relationship, and thus, our family.

After the graduation ceremony the next day, we gathered at the Bristol Bar & Grille and had a nice lunch together. Some of Randy's family joined us—his sisters Myrtle and Violet, and a couple of his nieces. My father was kind to them. He hugged them when we said our goodbyes. Randy was so happy I thought he might cry. I hated for him to get the wrong impression.

At home, we sat around the kitchen table talking about the excitement of the last few days. Tevin and Tyler told Grandpa Campion about the colleges they'd be going to in the fall. They expressed their excitement, their worries, and their doubts. Dad clapped each of them on the back and assured them they'd be fine.

Then suddenly, he raised a finger. "I have some things for you." He got up from the table and slipped into the bedroom, returning a few minutes later with two small but hefty gift bags. He handed one to each of the boys, along with a card. They opened the cards first, and their jaws dropped when they read the generous amount on the checks. Tyler threw his arms around Dad's neck. Tevin waited until his brother calmed down before giving Dad a more subdued but equally appreciative embrace. In his gift bag, Tevin found some books on John F. Kennedy to fuel his passion for writing. Tyler's was filled with music scripts and DVDs of classic musicals. As the boys showed off their gifts to one another, Randy and I moved in to thank my father.

"They've earned it," he replied, and as he gazed at the boys across the room, I could see that he sincerely loved them. And when he looked back at me, I thought there was something like pride in his eyes. "You've done a good job with those boys."

Outside the sky had gone pink, and soon Mackenzie and DeSean came to say goodnight to their grandfather. They had school the next day, and Grandpa Campion would be flying back to New York in the morning.

"It was good to see you." Kenzie sideways hugged him.

"Keep studying hard in school," Dad told her.

When the kids had gone upstairs to bed, Randy and I said our goodbyes as well.

"We appreciate you making the trip," Randy said, and he hugged my father without reservation, with both arms, the way I'd seen him hug his sisters. "You are always welcome here."

"I'm glad to have made it," Dad said. "Let me know when you all get up to New York again."

Randy's face sagged, and when he turned to me, and I knew he was being hopeful again, as though my father might yet have a change of heart. *After all*, he might've been thinking, *the world is changing.* His look said, *Your dad hugged me, and it was heartfelt.* For Randy, that hug was symbolic of something greater—a sign that my father embraced our relationship, which I knew not to be true.

"Tevin will drive you to the airport tomorrow. You'll be in good hands, Dad."

We embraced briefly, in the way of our family—a one-handed sports hug, our arms loosely draped across each other's back. It reminded me of better days, snowy Saturdays driving across upstate New York with the AM radio playing Lawrence Welk. I thought of big, fierce college basketball players thundering down the court, my father sitting next to me, both of us riveted by the game, our voices lost in the boom of cheering fans.

I hugged my father one last time, careful not to hold on too long, reminding myself this was the best it would ever be. This was as good as it would get.

14: Going Public

Randy

I was navigating the bottlenecks of the Watterson Expressway when I called Paul to let him know I had escaped the office. "On my way home now. Traffic's heavy."

"How was your day?" Paul wanted to know.

"Busy. I didn't think I'd ever get out of there. How was yours?"

"Not so bad with all the college stuff out of the way. Everything's set. All we have to do now is help them move."

It was early summer, mid-June. Paul was off work but, as our family's education expert, he had spent his spare time before summer break helping Tevin and Tyler make arrangements to start college. We would be transporting them to separate schools in August. The occasion brought to mind the boys' first day of kindergarten, their clean clothes and new shoes, their fresh faces gazing up at me. I remembered tearing up then and how I had hated letting them go.

Where had the years gone? I wondered. Now we were seeing them off to college. It seemed impossible. "I don't even want to think about that," I said, and I could feel my face heating up, my eyes watering.

"Oh my gosh, me either," Paul replied, a slight tremble in his voice.

I focused on the semi-truck ahead of me and wished it would merge into the right lane so that I could pass. "Anything else going on? What are the kids up to?" I asked to break the silence.

"They're swimming."

Suddenly I could hear kitchen noises in the background—the faucet running, the rattle of cooking utensils. "I'm making chicken and rice."

My sadness drifted away, at least for the moment. The best part of summer was coming home to Paul's home-cooked meals. My stomach rumbled. "Sounds good. I'm starving."

"And oh, yes, I almost forgot—we got an interesting message from Telly today." Telly was a friend from Northern Kentucky whom we had met through our niece, Tina.

"Oh yeah? What about?"

"He heard a couple of attorneys over on Frankfort Avenue are looking for a same-sex couple to join a lawsuit against Governor Beshear challenging the gay marriage ban."

"A lawsuit? Wow. We'll have to talk about that later."

"It might be worth looking into."

"Okay. I'm hopping off here. I'll see you in a few minutes."

"Be safe, Dad. Love you."

***

Later that evening before bed, Paul and I debriefed about the day's events. I reminded him of our earlier conversation while climbing under the covers. "So what about this message from Telly about a gay marriage lawsuit?"

Paul grabbed the remote from the nightstand and muted the TV. "It's two attorneys— Shannon Fauver and Dawn Elliot." He scrolled through his phone for details. "There are apparently two other couples involved. Remember Mike and Greg, who adopted two kids?"

I nodded.

They were married in Canada, and the other couple was married in the states. So now they're looking for a couple with children who got married in the states." He paused and looked up at me.

I recalled the upsetting turn of events in 2004, when Kentucky voters had approved the state version of the Defense of Marriage Act, which discriminated against gay couples by defining marriage as legal only if it was between a man and a woman.

"It's a lawsuit against Governor Beshear." Paul was nearly grinning.

"This is probably something we should do." I reclined onto my pillow. "It could be big. It could change things."

Paul lay on his side facing me, his head propped up on one elbow. "But it would mean putting ourselves out there in the public eye, making everything public." He was chewing his bottom lip. "That could also be big. It could blow up in our faces." He shuddered, and I knew he was thinking of the incident with a student's mother when he was teaching at Old Mill Elementary back when the twins were babies. "I just don't want any issues with parents."

I considered his point. We had worked tirelessly to blend in and not draw attention to ourselves—to live like a normal family. All our lives, our goal had been to keep our nontraditional family from becoming a topic—to keep our gay parenthood from becoming an issue, especially in the workplace. One thing Paul and I did not want was to have to deal with any drama over our "gay lifestyle." Joining the lawsuit would likely make some aspects of our careers more difficult. We would no longer be able to float around incognito.

"We should talk to the kids about it," I suggested.

"Good idea," he agreed, setting his phone on the nightstand and snuggling up next to me.

I hugged him closer. "I know it won't be easy, Dad, but I think it would set a good example for the kids for us to stand up for what we believe in."

Paul was silent for a minute. "Tevin and Tyler are adults, and Mackenzie and DeSean are practically grown. They would probably be fine with it. They've handled everything with such … " He paused, searching for the right word. "… with such grace."

I chuckled. "They're great kids. We're really blessed."

"Yep," he said simply, and he turned to me with a light shining in his eyes—not from the lamps or the TV, but a light from some other world. That look said everything. That look said it all.

I kissed his cheek. "You know, Mr. Campion, we got everything we ever hoped for, and we did it together. Everything except this." I sighed and looked up at the ceiling.

Paul clasped the arm I had draped over him, pressing it against his chest. My skin tingled from his touch.

"I guess this is it, then," he said, turning toward me, eyes still shining. "The moment we've been waiting for."

A chill came over me then, a full body shot of adrenaline. A voice whispered, *We can't lose.* I thought it was Paul, but his lips never moved. Maybe I imagined it. Maybe it was the voice of God.

***

The next evening, before the kids could break away from the dinner table, we brought up the idea of joining the legal battle for marriage equality in Kentucky.

"It could end up becoming a really big deal," I explained. "But our big worry is the effect it will have on you all."

Paul propped his elbows on the kitchen table and folded his hands in front of him. "We could become news items. Our whole family. We might be scrutinized. There's probably going to be media attention." He wanted the children to understand the significance of the decision.

I leaned forward. "So what do you all think?"

Tevin glanced at his siblings before speaking up. "I think it's a great idea," he said. "It's an important issue, and it's worth any hostility we might come up against."

"I think you should go for it!" Tyler flashed us his stage grin and assumed a dancer's stance with his chest sticking out, fists planted on hips. "We'll all be superstars," he added, wiggling his eyebrows for dramatic effect.

We all laughed.

"Seriously, though, are you guys okay with this?"

DeSean shrugged. "Sure. Why not?"

Mackenzie was squirming in her seat. She bobbed her head up and down while watching her brothers, as though urging them to hurry up and give their consent in unison. "Can I go swimming now?" she wanted to know.

Paul rolled his eyes and patted her back. "Now hold on, Kenzie."

I waved a hand to dismiss them. "I think the consensus is pretty clear, Dad."

Everyone exploded from the table.

***

On a muggy afternoon in early August, I met Paul after work at the attorneys' office on Frankfort Avenue. It was an old, three-story Victorian house near Story Avenue on the eastern edge of downtown Louisville, an eclectic neighborhood with an outdoor flea market, an arts center with galleries and studios, a small theater, and mostly family-owned shops and restaurants. A sign taped to the front door of the attorneys' office read, "Clients seen by appointment only. Please ring bell."

Paul looked at me with raised eyebrows. I shrugged and pressed the brass button on the doorframe. The doorbell made an old-timey, gong-like noise. A minute after it tolled, we heard the snap and slide of a deadbolt unlocking, and a young woman appeared.

"Randy Johnson and Paul Campion. We have an appointment."

The woman nodded once and opened the door, leading us into the foyer, where I immediately noticed a row of chairs blocking the bottom of a winding staircase.

After locking the door behind us, the assistant showed us through the hallway into what appeared to be a living room, with couches, bookshelves, a fireplace in one corner, and a big conference table in the middle. With its everyday furnishings, the space had a homey, lived-in feel. I noticed some schoolbooks on an end table.

"Shannon and Dawn will be right with you," the assistant said and left.

We sat down at the conference table. Through a doorway off one side of the room, I could see a kitchen; on the opposite side directly off the conference room was an office, the door slightly ajar, muffled voices coming from inside. Next to it was another office with an open pocket door, the desk inside piled high with folders, books, and papers. I had no sooner noticed the office when a tall, smiling woman emerged from behind the stacks and entered the room.

"Paul and Randy?" she inquired, one hand pressed delicately to her sternum, and strode across the room easily in high heels.

We got up from the table. "Yes," I said, extending my hand.

She made her way toward us, tossed a folder onto the table, and transitioned quickly from a handshake to a hug. She had a floral, musky scent. "I am so happy to meet you both. Dawn Elliott," she said, turning to Paul and embracing him, as well.

Shannon followed, as though on cue, in a navy pants suit and eggshell blouse. She had loose, shoulder-length hair, and she spoke rapidly, which made her a bit difficult to understand. She shook our hands and invited us to have a seat.

"So let us fill you in on the case," Shannon said, placing her palms on the shiny tabletop. She recounted the history of how they began working with a lesbian couple, Kim and Tammy, who lived on the outskirts of Louisville in Shelby County, about challenging the state's marriage ban. She talked so fast that her words were sometimes muddled. I had to ask for clarification at least once.

"Kim and Tammy wanted to get Kentucky to recognize that they're married," Shannon explained. "And they wanted us to represent them, so we got them jumpstarted on the paperwork. But while that was held up in processing, another couple came forward, Greg and Mike, who got married in Canada back in—when was that, Dawn?"

Dawn flipped through her folder, ran a finger down and across a couple documents. "Here it is," she said. "That was 2004."

"Yes, 2004," Shannon said, turning back to us. "So, with Greg and Mike's case, we have the question of whether Kentucky has to recognize a marriage performed in another country. With you two involved, we have a stronger case—a couple with children who were married within the United States. It's going to be a little easier to argue, I think."

Paul and I looked at each other. She made it sound as though we had already agreed to be part of the case.

Shannon seemed to read my mind. "You are in, aren't you? We're doing this to advance the same-sex marriage issue. We just need you to be the faces to the case. The only expense for the plaintiffs are the filing fees."

I glanced at Paul. "What do you think, Dad? Are we in?"

He shrugged and smiled. "Why not?"

Dawn clapped her hands. "Hell, yes!" she exclaimed, her laughter filling the room.

15: Standing Up for Love

Paul

Not long after meeting with the attorneys for Kentucky's marriage equality case, we weighed the pros and cons of being part of the lawsuit over dinner at home one evening. I was having second thoughts. I feared the exposure for Randy and me, especially in our jobs. I thought about my role as counselor at Shelby Traditional and the likelihood that one of the school's 700 students would see us on TV or hear about our involvement in the case. In the age of social media, rumors spread quickly, and I knew it would only be a matter of time before unhappy parents stormed the school, questioning my qualifications and the impact of my corruptive "homosexual lifestyle" on their children.

When we finished eating, the kids scattered, and Randy and I remained at the table talking about the surge in teen suicides amid cyberbullying over sexual identity.

"I think we have a moral imperative on our hands," Randy said, and the way he said it, in that thick southern drawl of his, made me grin.

"You sound like one of those TV preachers," I teased.

"Real funny, Dad." His turquoise eyes narrowed at me for an instant, and then he quickly recaptured the conversation. "The depression and anxiety these young people are dealing with these days, it's scary." He threw out his hands. "I've been through all that. We both went through it."

I cringed at the thought of those days. "I can't imagine how much worse things are now with the Internet and social media." As a teacher and a counselor, I'd witnessed the disturbing trends and treatment of LGBTQ youth, the public shaming and backbiting that stemmed from sheer ignorance and outright fear.

Randy's voice softened. "And kids are plugged in twenty-four seven, so they're constantly being bombarded with this stuff."

I thought back on the covert conflicts I experienced as a gay youth involved in sports. Would our involvement in this case be worth the risks?

***

On a snowy Saturday morning in 1984, I arrived at the Jamestown High School gymnasium for basketball practice bundled in a red-and-green letterman's jacket and the invisible cloak I'd been wearing since childhood. It was a cloak that veiled my sexuality, that kept me safe from emotional and physical abuse. I had never been bullied for being gay, but I had witnessed the prejudice and persecution of those who were different, and I had lived in constant fear of being found out.

Inside the gym, I stopped to shake off some snow and blink away the brightness of the outside world. I was in my usual sleepy state, and I yawned and stretched slightly before throwing my duffle bag over my shoulder and trudging along the sideline of the basketball court to the locker room. My coach sat on the bleachers scribbling on a clipboard, and I waved at him before ducking into the tricky territory of high testosterone and budding male bodies. The air was thick with the musky scent of Old Spice and the rattle and clang of locker doors opening and closing. I greeted my teammates with the usual round of "Heys" and stepped carefully across floor tiles that were slick with melted snow brought in on shoe bottoms.

Spotting an open bench seat near the back, I made a half-hearted attempt to perk up for practice, imagining myself executing a complicated play with a crazy sprint pattern to avoid the arms and elbows crowding the locker area. It was a diversionary tactic, too, to keep myself focused on the game, rather than ogling the army of young, half-naked men who, unlike me, appeared completely at ease in their new hairy skin.

After dodging through the throng of bodies, I collapsed onto the bench with a sigh. Everyone was moaning and groaning about having to get up so early or discussing their Friday night escapades.

"Hey, did ya hear about Bobby Stevens getting a piece of ass?" Dominic called out to no one in particular, pulling a clean white T-shirt over his curly mop.

All eyes turned to Bobby, the shortest and most freckled member of the team, who was hiding behind his locker door, shaking his head and grinning.

"No kidding!" Brad cried. "The last virgin at Jamestown High?"

Howling laughter filled the locker room. I joined in, wrapped in my secret cloak to blend in with the straight guys, although I felt awful about the language they were using, and I pitied Bobby Stevens, regardless how good of a sport he was being. His face was flushed, and he looked as though he was trying to squeeze inside his locker and disappear.

Dominic nodded, his mouth bent in a half smirk. "Yeah, I saw him at the drugstore buying condoms."

Jack was lacing up his sneakers, one foot hiked on the bench. "Musta been Patti Michaels. She'd do anybody." he said with a wink and switched feet.

I flinched and scooted down the bench. It felt as though someone was pulling at my cloak.

"Come on, now," Dominic interjected. "He's got himself a good girl. Suzie Taylor."

"Oh, Suzie Taylor… " someone chided. "How much did you pay her, Bobby? Did she give you a blow job, too, or did that cost extra?"

The cloak-pulling turned into insistent tugging. I felt vulnerable there, amid the guffawing that echoed within the cinder block walls. Jimmy, another teammate, might have laughed a little longer than the rest of them. Whatever the case, Brad took the opportunity to engage in what was commonly considered friendly banter.

"Hey, Jimmy," he said, stuffing his black duffle bag in a locker and slamming the door harder than necessary to draw everyone's attention, not just Jimmy's.

Jimmy was already moving for the exit. He stopped and spun around, his lanky arms spread open in a questioning manner, as though he had already been accused of something. "Yeah?"

Brad chuckled, tilting his head back as he pointed at him. "I saw you coming out of Big Mike's last night!"

The locker room exploded with laughter. Big Mike's was a gay bar in town. I had never been there. Probably none of us had. Most of us were under eighteen, the legal drinking age. Still, the guys on the team routinely accused one another of frequenting the place. I fretted at the very real possibility of a finger being pointed at me. I bowed my head and folded my arms over my chest, hoping to stay shrouded.

Jimmy held up the middle fingers of both hands and shouted above the roar. "Fuck you, Brad!"

A chorus of "woo hoos" accompanied by jeers followed.

Brad's tongue hung from his mouth and his hand flew to his crotch and made a pumping motion while his hips thrust back and forth suggestively.

By now I had slid down the bench a good way and was busying myself getting dressed. I felt naked at that moment—felt as though the cloak had been stripped away. My head pounded, and my stomach twisted in fear. I reached into the depths of my mind's eye and pulled the cloak up over my head.

When I looked up, the locker room was empty.

*

I was attracted to guys at a young age, but, of course, I never acted on those impulses. They were unspoken fantasies—some strange phase I was going through, that I thought I would outgrow. While my brothers were sweet on Ginger on the TV show "Gilligan's Island," I had a secret crush on the olive-skinned Professor in his crisp white shirt. When my friends were plastering their bedroom walls with Charlie's Angels posters, I was privately fantasizing about Chachi from "Happy Days." I was deeply ashamed of my desires, yet I could not suppress them.

In my teenage years, no one made fun of the way I looked or the friends I hung out with. I was the quintessential Catholic boy, the youngest of eight children, with neatly combed, barbershop-cut hair, usually dressed in a polo shirt and Levis. When I was eleven years old, I became an altar boy, following in the footsteps of my five brothers. I was popular at school, an athlete and an honor roll student. Further masking my sexuality, I always had a girlfriend, although I never managed to fall in love with any of them, let alone get past the necking and petting stage. That worried me.

Friends and family saw me as an all-American boy, destined for happiness and success. Although I did my best to maintain that persona, I felt trapped and confused hiding beneath that good-boy cloak. Homosexuality was not discussed at church or at home. My parents believed in blind obedience to our faith, which meant following very narrow rules without question. I learned that words such as "liberal" and "free thinker" carried an evil connotation.

In those angst-ridden years, I felt I could never throw off the secret cloak, that the true Paul Campion would remain forever an eleven-year-old altar boy ready to recite the Act of Contrition, the Hail Mary, the Our Father.

O my God, I am heartfully sorry for having offended thee, and I detest all my sins because of Thy just punishment, but most of all because I have offended Thee my God, Who is all good and deserving of all my love. I firmly resolve, with the help of Thy grace, to sin no more, and to avoid the near occasion of sin. Amen.

The older I got, the greater my attraction to the same sex grew, and the more the good-boy cloak seemed to shrink. Wherever I could find privacy, I cried to God, *Please don't allow me to have these feelings. Please make them go away.* Many times, I contemplated suicide. In tenth grade, I had a brief respite when I found an outlet for my emotions through writing, courtesy of a spirited English teacher named Ms. Whitehead. She was a short-haired, matronly woman with a contagious laugh, and I looked forward to her class, and even the class discussions, which I shunned in other subjects. Ms. Whitehead's class was different—from the physical layout of the room, which was arranged in learning pods designed for interaction rather than rows of desks, to the energy that embodied the space—a space that felt safe and engaging. The walls were covered with posters of famous authors and classic poetry, and the noise level was louder than other classrooms, and filled with the excited chatter of teenagers and the constant screech of pods and chairs being shifted.

Our class discussions were progressive and open and usually revolved around teenagers' struggles and experiences. Like the class discussions, Ms. Whitehead's assignments worked mainly to build confidence in us and foster respect for one another. One of our assignments was to write a poem. Mine was not the best quality in terms of technique, but I recall pouring my heart into those lines and somehow conveying my feelings without giving myself away. The words expressed my desire to start my life all over. I believe Ms.

Whitehead read between the lines and understood my struggle. She returned it to me with a note that read:

> *You have an amazing life ahead of you.... You are the author of your life.*

I'm not sure what happened to that poem, but I read Ms. Whitehead's note many times in the weeks and months—maybe years—that followed. In my darkest moments, her words were like a salve to me. Perhaps they saved my life.

*

On the basketball court, I excelled. I expressed a passion like no other. I loved the game, and I had the skills and the competitive spirit of a good athlete. Still, basketball was part of my sham, my disguise. As long as I succeeded on the court, it would detract attention from the real me, and it would distract me from the inner turmoil I was experiencing. As long as I could gain the praise of my coach, my teammates, and my friends, I could shield myself from any speculation about the real Paul Campion.

As I headed out to the court, fear wracked my body. I was no longer sleepy but on high alert and ready to hustle. I had to. I had to deflect the negative thoughts. I had to impress my coach with my speed, astonish my teammates with an amazing pass. This was how I redeemed myself. It was how I survived.

After practice that snowy Saturday and the incident in the locker room, I shriveled back inside my secret cloak, alternately hating myself and hating the world I lived in, tearfully attempting to pray away my feelings. My friends talked about masturbating with girly magazines or by thinking of specific girls we knew at school, but I had no such thoughts when pleasuring myself. Instead I thought of Pete Cochrane from the TV show "The Mod Squad" or one of the striking young men who worked at the shopping mall. I doubted that God would change me, or could change me. This was some sort of punishment. It was hell on earth.

At home, I locked myself in the bathroom and prayed the Hail Mary.

Hail Mary, full of grace. Our Lord is with thee. Blessed art thou among women, and blessed is the fruit of thy womb, Jesus. Holy Mary, Mother of God, pray for us sinners, now and at the hour of our death. Amen.

I was overwhelmed with guilt and shame. The tears wouldn't stop. I contemplated the sleeping pills in the medicine cabinet, wondered whether I could swallow enough to find peace, wondered how long it would take before eternal sleep washed over me.

Ending my life seemed the only way out. After much sobbing and deliberating, I decided it was a justifiable choice. I reasoned that I would not only end my suffering, but I would keep myself from violating my faith and going against God's will. That day I decided that after high school, I would either shed the cloak or end my own life. Both options terrified me, but the pain of living day to day was often that unbearable. The cloak was suffocating me.

I tucked the sleeping pills back inside the medicine cabinet and splashed my face with cold water. I had options now. I would not go on this way. I couldn't.

***

It seemed impossible that the gay rights movement had come so far, while fear and hatred persisted. As Randy and I were discussing the lawsuit, I scanned a story on my phone about the conservative right's longstanding practice of so-called conversion therapy—a highly damaging attempt to break gay and lesbian youth of their "deviant sexual behavior." The practice had come under fire in recent headlines, with New York, New Jersey, and California attempting to ban licensed therapists from using the method.

I caught myself chewing my thumbnail and set down my phone. "I dread the backlash," I admitted. "For me, it's not so much my principal or the teachers or any of my coworkers really, but the parents."

"I know," Randy replied. "Things could get ugly." He patted my back and gathered some of the dinner dishes. "I'm also worried about those ladies doing all the legal work for free. It could take months, maybe even years to get our case heard. That's a lot of time and energy to put into something without getting paid," he said, rinsing the plates in the sink.

"They understand what's at stake, just like we do," I reasoned, getting up to help clear the table. "We've been making financial sacrifices all our lives. Look at our health insurance premiums." I started loading the dishwasher. "And who's a better example than me to prove the importance of having it?" I didn't like to talk about my prostate cancer. I didn't like to think of those words, let alone say them out loud.

"That's true," Randy agreed. "And we've made other sacrifices, too. We've done our part over the years. You know what? I think we just have to let Dawn and Shannon do the work now and trust that they know what they're getting into."

I shifted the plates on the bottom rack and adjusted the cups and glasses on top. He was right, of course. We had invested extra time in raising our children due to legal barriers that kept both of us from being listed as parents on their adoption papers. We had suffered emotionally from being treated like second-class citizens. We had faced discrimination with our children watching. We had never planned to become activists, but we couldn't allow unfair practices to hurt our family.

✳✳✳

We had taken a stand for injustice when the twins were seven years old, while we were living in Old Louisville. Through our friends Jeanie and Shawn, we learned that the Louisville YMCA had narrowed its definition of family to "legally married couples" and was denying family memberships to gay couples who couldn't be married legally under Kentucky law. We had been active members of the Y for a few years by then, enrolling the boys in seasonal sports such as soccer and T-ball through the Northeast branch. I coached youth soccer and basketball leagues, and I used the gym downtown to work out several times a week.

When I heard about the policy change, I was rattled. "We have to join the boycott," I told Randy. "This is demoralizing to our family. We shouldn't have to pay as individuals."

He agreed without question.

On a warm spring day while the four of us sat on our deck, I explained to Tevin and Tyler that they would not be participating in soccer through the Y. "We'll try to find another league for you to play in."

Tyler shrugged. He was more interested in sailing his Pikachu toy through the air than he was in discussing summer sports options.

Tevin, however, was his usual reflective self. He remembered the oath that the YMCA required team players to recite before each game. "We have to say that pledge. We have to promise to be a team player and to treat each other with respect," he said, looking out thoughtfully over the back yard. "But they're not playing fair at all."

I was amazed that Tevin had held onto those words and could relate the values that the oath conveyed in another context. I patted his back. "You're right, son."

"It should be the same for everybody," he added.

Randy's eyes widened, and he jerked back in a startled gesture. "He sounds just like you, Dad," he said.

I chuckled and nodded. "You're a wise young man, Tevin."

Two months later, the Fairness Campaign organized a protest to pressure the Louisville YMCA into revising its membership policy. The weekend before the protest, our friends Jeanie and Shawn came over with their daughter Mahala to help make signs that read "Y Discriminate?" Jeanie and Randy arranged stools around the kitchen island and organized the markers and stencils. The kids worked on one sign, and the adults worked on another. While Randy and Jeanie oversaw the sign-making process, Shawn and I chatted about running. We were both teachers and had the summer off.

"Let's meet up at Cherokee for a run this weekend," Shawn suggested, combing her bangs back with her fingers. She had a short, sensible hairstyle and an easygoing personality. I admired her athleticism and was motivated by her energy.

"Sounds good. Maybe we could take the kids swimming at the Bubble afterward."

The kids punched their fists in the air and shouted their approval.

Shawn turned up her palms. "I guess that was decided."

"Maybe we should see how the sign turns out," Jeanie proposed, winking at Shawn.

The children groaned collectively. Shoulders slumped. Eyes rolled.

Mahala propped an elbow up on the counter and sighed. "I'm getting tired."

Jeanie leaned over and kissed Mahala's head. "We're almost finished, honey."

After a few minutes, Tyler dropped his marker on the counter and leaped off his stool. "I'm done!" he announced. "Can we go play on the trampoline now?" He pressed his palms together, as though praying for permission to escape this mundane, grown-up chore.

"Let's finish this first," Randy replied, tapping the poster board with his finger.

Jeanie helped him back onto the stool and pointed at the fuzzy blue markings he had made. "You're doing great, Tyler. I think you need a little more here."

Tevin ran a finger under the giant lettering and sounded out "discriminate." He looked at Mahala and Tyler. "It means not playing fair."

Tyler made long, hurried strokes with his marker, uninterested in his brother's explanation.

Tevin nudged him. "That's why we can't play soccer."

"I know that," Tyler said, scratching his nose.

"Because the Y discriminates. They say we're not a family." Tevin turned to me for affirmation.

I nodded and rubbed the short, thick rug on top of Tevin's head. Here was a loving boy with a keen sense of right and wrong. If only the rest of society could see the issue so clearly. Suddenly I thought of Jesus telling his disciples, "Whoever does not receive the kingdom of God like a child shall not enter it."

I said a silent prayer for the boys, for Mahala, for all the children who suffered the repercussions of an intolerant world. I stood between Tevin and Tyler and rested my hands on their shoulders. These were my sons. We were a family. This would become my mantra in the days ahead of us, in fighting for the right to be a father, a caregiver of the highest order.

A few days later, we loaded up our signs and drove downtown to the protest in front of the YMCA building. Randy met us there. He was usually the outspoken one, but when the opportunity presented itself, I took the bullhorn.

"This is my family. We are a family." My voice was strong and steady. Randy and the boys stood next to me, and as I looked at them, I felt anger for all the unfair treatment we had endured over the years, and for the threat of bigoted rules and regulations that would dare to define us differently—as something less than a family, as though we were unworthy of that status. "And we do not intend to have our family sitting in the back of the bus." The words rose up like fire, like the heat of the early summer sun on the pavement. "We demand that the YMCA recognize us for who we are—a family—rather than define us in a way that's narrow and offensive."

The crowd applauded and cheered. Tevin and Tyler smiled up at me, clapping along with the others. I handed off the bullhorn and hugged the twins at my waist. Randy grinned at me and joined us for a group hug. The atmosphere was festive. People rode by honking their horns in support. Everyone exiting the building gave us a thumbs-up or cheered. It felt good to take a stand, and to have so many standing with us. It felt magical, like anything was possible in that moment. And why shouldn't it? I thought. Love was a powerful thing.

***

Randy retreated to the office to take care of the bills, and I finished putting away the leftovers. I knew he was right about trusting Dawn and Shannon, but I had my reservations.

The words of Solomon under the influence of the Holy Spirit came to mind: *Trust in the Lord with all thine heart, and lean not unto thine own understanding.* I had long questioned the purpose of our suffering, and this Proverb reminded me that God had a plan. Slowly, I talked myself off the ledge of disbelief and back into the fire of life and love. I thought of all we had endured over the years and the fate of those we would leave in the hands of the world, the fate of all God's children. As a school counselor, I was aware of the surge in suicides among gay and lesbian youth, and I knew that I had to do everything in my power to defeat that trend. Surely we were working for the greater good—for a higher purpose and a higher power and a better future.

I loaded the dirty utensils, filled the soap container, and pushed the start button. How I wished the rest of world could operate so easily. The YMCA had ended up changing its policy to be inclusive of gay couples and their families within a few months of the protest. We had the opportunity to initiate a change that would help families like ours and ease the burden for LGBTQ teenagers. Was our involvement in the marriage equality lawsuit worth the risks? I asked myself, and the answer came easily. Yes, indeed. It most certainly was.

Clockwise from top: Paul in high school, 1983; Randy in college, 1991; new dads at Lourdes Hospital in Paducah, KY, February 23, 1995

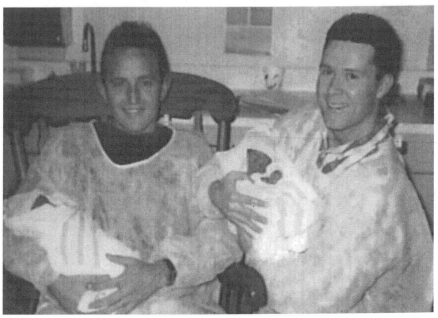

*Clockwise from top: Mamaw
Frances with Tevin; Daddy Randy
with Tyler; Daddy Randy with
Tyler & Daddy Paul with Tevin
after their Baptism, 1995*

Clockwise from top: Grandma Campion with Tevin; Grandpa Campion with Tevin; Daddy Paul with Tyler & Great-Grandma Patterson with Tevin

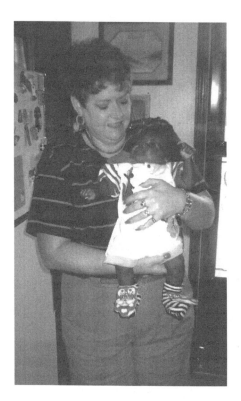

*Top: Aunt Mo
with Tevin;
Aunt Vi with
Tyler*

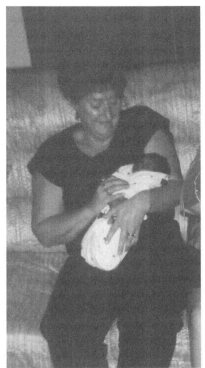

*Top: Aunt Katie with Tyler;
Uncle Mike with Tevin,
Mackenzie, and Tyler*

*Top: Daddy
Paul reading to
Tevin and Tyler,
1997; Tevin and
Tyler, 1998*

The Johnson-Campion Family, 2001

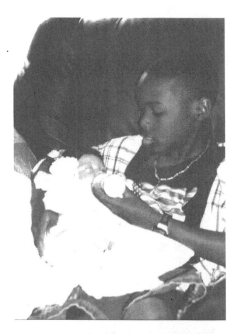

Clockwise from top: Tyler
with Mackenzie, 2003;
Mackenzie, 2004; The
Johnson-Campion kids,
2007; Mackenzie, 2008

From top: DeSean, 2008;
DeSean, Mackenzie, Tevin,
and Tyler; The Johnson-
Campion Family, 2008

Clockwise from top: The Johnson-Campion kids, 2010; Family vacation, 2009; Mackenzie, 2011

*Clockwise from top: Paul and
Randy, 2015; Tyler, 2012;
DeSean, 2012*

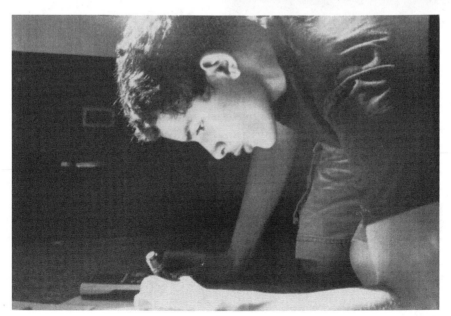

131

Top: Tevin on MSNBC, April 2015; Tevin, DeSean, Mackenzie, Randy, and Paul outside the Supreme Court Building on the day of the oral arguments for Obergefell v. Hodges

16: Separation Anxiety

Paul

Not long after graduation, Tevin had started sorting through clothes and boxing up books and other belongings, completely unaided, without any prompting from Randy or me. I had no doubt he would be ready to move to Berea College at the end of August.

Meanwhile, Tyler had done nothing to prepare for dorm life at the College Conservatory of Music at the University of Cincinnati other than forge online friendships with future classmates. He was part of an exclusive group of twenty new freshmen selected for the musical theatre class from over 850 applicants through a rigorous process that had included auditions. The students had found each other on social networking sites and had been sharing their excitement and enthusiasm for attending the prestigious school while getting to know each other's tastes and interests.

I spent all summer trying to persuade Tyler to organize and pack. I brought him boxes and picked up new linens and kitchen utensils. "You need to get started, Ty," I told him as I surveyed the contents of his bedroom; several stacks of clean laundry, books, DVDs, and dance shoes that were strewn about his bedroom.

The next day, I repeated my suggestion. "Tevin's practically finished and you haven't even started," I pointed out.

"I know, I know. I'll do it tonight," Tyler promised, with little enthusiasm in his voice, secretly rolling his eyes to amuse his sister, who was watching him demonstrate a new tap routine on the patio. "That reminds me, Dad," he said, raising a finger. "I need to get new tap shoes."

"Okay, we'll do that tomorrow," I said and turned to go inside. "As long as you get started packing."

"Oh, and Dad," he called after me, batting his eyes and flashing his stage smile. "I need new dance shoes, too." In typical Tyler fashion, he did a hop shuffle and flung his arm out dramatically.

I stopped long enough to clap and assure him we'd get the shoes he needed. I shook my head, chuckling to myself. While college freshmen across the country obsessed over clothes, computers, and basic necessities for being on their own for the first time in their lives, our kid had only one concern: dance shoes. It seemed a symbolic way to prepare to make his way into the world, to get on his feet. I wished I had been as carefree when I was his age. I wished that I had had the footing and self-confidence he would be starting out with. I was glad he had that advantage. Although I hadn't been as mentally prepared as Tyler, moving on from high school to college had been liberating for me.

***

After graduating high school, I didn't immediately come out as gay, but I did find refuge in Jamestown's underground of gay bars. I was taking classes at the community college and hanging out with many of the same high school friends. On weekends, we gathered at the Rusty Nail for a few drinks. One night I got enough liquid courage in me to make my way to Doc's.

"I'm calling it a night," I told the crew and downed the last of my beer before shoving back from the table.

"Already?" someone asked. "It's still early!"

"Leave him alone. Can't you see the man's drunk?"

I shrugged off their snickering.

"Goodnight, Paul. Stay on your side of the sidewalk."

"And don't pick up any strangers on the way home!"

I shook my head and smiled back at them as I made my way to the exit.

Outside the sky was clear, the moon burning high in the west, a sprinkling of stars visible in spite of the streetlights. The air was cool enough for a jacket, and I instantly wished I had relieved my bladder before rushing out the door. But I was too nervous to go back inside, so I kept walking through the parking lot toward the street. I strode the sidewalk in the direction of Doc's, all the while wondering how I would approach the massive granite building on Pine Street without being seen. I had heard about the bar and knew it was located in the basement, and that somewhere within the building's vast commercial space was a doctor's office.

When I was within a few blocks, I surveyed the streets and dodged behind trees and into the shadows to avoid being seen by oncoming traffic. By the time I arrived, I needed to urinate so badly that I wasted little time getting in the door. Once inside, my heart seemed to drop into my stomach. At first, I was so tense that nothing seemed to register. I stood at the entrance wiping my feet over and over on the door mat, as though waiting for someone to come and greet me, although the last thing I wanted at that moment was to be approached. I just wanted to wade into these strange, new waters on my own terms and gradually work my way up to swimming.

After a few minutes, my nerves calmed enough for me to move forward and take in the unusual ambiance of the place. The low lighting was typical for a bar, but the subdued noise level and modern décor surprised me. There were leather chairs and mahogany tables, and people were moving about slowly, if at all. Most were seated at tables, engaged in conversation. Some were holding hands. It seemed more like a rich man's living room than what I had imagined a gay bar would be like.

I eased along the wall and stood there alone, trying to watch without watching, which was awkward. I scanned every space and corner until I spotted a cubby that appeared to be a restroom, and I moved with newfound purpose in that direction. The restroom was as plush as the rest of the place, with a marble sink and polished brass faucet. I glimpsed my reflection in the mirror and worried whether I might be underdressed.

When I returned to the bar area, I recognized a group of girls from high school at a table near the dance floor. One of them, a short, pretty brunette I remembered from English class, smiled in my direction. She said something to the others, and a few of them looked back at me and nodded. The music seemed a bit louder now, although I didn't see a deejay. A couple of men eyed me as they walked past. One raised an eyebrow in mock surprise. My beer buzz from earlier had begun to wear off. I was considering buying a drink when the pretty brunette walked up.

"Paul?" she said, tilting her head as though to get a better look at me. "That's your name, right?"

"Yeah," I managed, clearing my throat. "Sorry."

She spun around and gave some sort of signal to her friends, then turned back to me. "We went to Jamestown High together. Class of Eighty-four?" She grinned, revealing a row of shiny white teeth. "Actually, we all did," she added, gesturing toward the girls at the table.

I nodded and smiled back. "Are you a ... you know?"

"A lesbian?" She giggled behind her hand. "No. You don't have to be gay or lesbian to come here. It's a lot of fun. Come on over and join us."

And before I knew it, she had me by the arm and was leading me to their table.

Her name was Tammy, and after she introduced me to everyone, we ordered drinks and talked about our high school days two years before and what we were doing with our lives.

"Are you coming out?" Tammy asked me at one point.

"Not yet," I replied quickly, chewing my lip. "But hopefully. One day."

After being initiated by a group of straight girls, what I found at a gay bar was a community of individuals who had experiences similar to mine. The underground was a different world, a place where we were all accepted, where absolute love and life were possible.

After that night, I started frequenting Doc's once a month. Soon the infamous Big Mike's, the bar that my high school teammates had joked about, also became part of my secret gay life repertoire. Big Mike's was at the corner of a busy and well-lit intersection, so it was somewhat trickier to navigate. I would park my parents' mammoth Delta 88 two blocks away and dart through the busy streets, ducking into the shadows or hiding behind utility poles when cars were coming as I did when approaching Doc's. I moved like a spy and became even more nimble in those days than I had been on the basketball court in high school.

While I had discovered an oasis in Jamestown where I was free to be myself, I had not yet officially come out as gay. I sometimes ran into the men and women I met in the underground when I was with my straight friends and family members, and I lived in constant fear that the quiet nods and casual "hellos" we tossed to one another would arouse their suspicions. What would I say if my mother took notice of me nodding to a stranger at the shopping mall and asked, "Who was that man, Paul? And how do you know him?" The sheer thought of such a confrontation made my heart race and my stomach knot up. I couldn't lie to her. I had been raised to believe lying only made matters worse.

When I moved fifty miles away to attend St. Bonaventure University, I was still grappling with my sexuality and my spirituality. My first semester there, I felt a calling to go to church services every day at noon. I remember especially the peak of fall, when the oaks and maples turned, their foliage a magnificent and fiery display across the campus. I trekked through their beauty from my dormitory to the church, which at that time of day was filled with nuns and townies, rather than students. The church held the usual furnishings—pews and altar, a lectern and organ, a crucifix, a tabernacle. There were stained glass windows, votive candles, the Stations of the Cross. There was nothing extraordinary that was visible to the naked eye, but something was at work inside me. On those occasions, I felt a special connection with the Blessed Virgin, and I would often recite the Hail Mary.

> *Hail Mary, full of grace. Our Lord is with thee. Blessed art thou among women,   and blessed is the fruit of thy womb, Jesus. Holy Mary, Mother of God, pray for us sinners, now and at the hour of our death. Amen.*

It was during this change of seasons that I also had the chance to speak with the friars about my spiritual dilemma. I confided to one friar, "I'm gay, but my faith is important to me. I don't know how to reconcile the two."

He replied without hesitation. "There is nothing to reconcile, my son. You are who God wants you to be."

It was a clear and simple message, yet its power was immense, and the relief I felt at that moment is impossible to describe in words. A well sprang open inside me and the tears came at once, heavy and cleansing, clearing my mind of the doubt and the fear. It was the answer to all my childhood worries, everything I had been praying for since I was ten years old.

***

The night before we moved Tyler to Cincinnati, Randy and I were rooting through laundry baskets, folding our son's clothes, and organizing towels and toiletries in plastic milk crates. Tyler was emptying the shelves and drawers in his bedroom, deciding what to take and what to leave behind, launching a full-blown discussion on each pair of socks, every hat, every dance video he might need while he was away.

"You're going to have to figure it out a lot faster or you'll be up all night doing this," Randy warned him.

Tyler made a sad face and blinked at us. He got up from the floor. "I think that's all I need from in here," he said, closing the drawer he was working on and moving to the closet. He pulled out a dozen pairs of jeans and slacks and at least half the shirts he owned, leaving the finer clothes that were prone to wrinkling on their hangers and packing the rest in the extra-large suitcase sprawled open across his bed.

We left early the next morning. The hour-and-a-half drive to Cincinnati was uneventful, and we easily located the high-rise dormitory where Tyler would be staying right off Calhoun Street, the campus' main drag. In the cul-de-sac area just down the hill from Siddall Hall, we had to wait until another student's family returned one of the big carts designated for hauling personal belongings to dorm rooms. It was moving day not only for freshmen but also for student athletes. Navigating the loaded cart along the busy walkways and through the crowded hallways was a bit of a struggle. Afterward we had to wait for an elevator. Once on the eighth floor, we wheeled the cart to Tyler's room, which seemed even smaller than I remembered the dorm rooms being at St. Bonaventure. There were two desks and two stripped down twin-sized beds—one near the window, the other near the door.

"Since your roommate's not here yet, you get to pick beds. Which one do you want?" I asked. "We can help you get it made up."

An unfamiliar female voice came from the doorway. "Tyler? Is that you?"

Tyler spun around and cried out at the sight of his new friend. "Oh my God! I can't believe it!"

"Me either! You made it! We made it!"

The two of them embraced and broke into song, their voices harmonizing remarkably well. Randy looked at me. I shrugged and smiled. And so it went for the next half hour, Randy and I trying desperately to get Tyler organized, and Tyler flitting about the dorm, pecking out text messages and wandering off to greet each new classmate who entered the building.

Randy pointed at the cart. "Where's he going to put all this stuff?"

"I don't know." I opened up one of the closet doors and started hanging up some of his clothes.

When Tyler came back into the room, we bombarded him. "Where do you want to put your coffeemaker?" "How about your toiletries?" "Did you pick which bed you want yet?"

For a few minutes, he worked with us to unload the cart, make his bed, and arrange some items on one of the desks, but soon another distraction carried him out the door. Randy and I finally gave up. We waited until the squeals of delight and laughter died down in the hallway before wrangling Tyler back into the room and announcing our departure.

"Let's get a quick picture at your desk," Randy insisted, and Tyler sat down and posed while Dad snapped the photo.

"Are you all set? Do you have everything you need?" I asked.

Tyler scanned the room and grabbed the cart handle. "Will you take this down with you?"

Randy took hold of the cart and turned it around.

Tyler hugged us both. "Thank you for bringing me, and thank you for all your help."

"We love you, son." Randy said.

"Love you, too." He smiled, already moving toward the door where a few of his friends were lingering.

Randy maneuvered the cart and I walked just ahead of him, glancing over my shoulder before we rounded the corner to the elevator. By now Tyler was lost in conversation with his classmates. We could hear them chattering right up until the elevator doors closed. It was painful leaving without him. Unlike the ride to campus, which had been filled with his passion and energy, the ride home was devoid of his presence. It was a long, quiet drive. Randy stared straight ahead, but I could hear him sniffling. I found some Kleenex in the glove box and handed him one. He thanked me. I patted his leg and tried not to think about what had just happened. How our baby boy had slipped through our hands. How overnight he had become a grown man.

***

Before graduating from college, I started telling my closest friends, one at a time, that I was gay. I knew there would be repercussions, but the liberation for me was more important. Most responded with grace and kindness, assuring me our friendship would not change. Over time, others outside of my close circle learned that I was gay, and while most were accepting, some were not. I quickly learned to let go of those friendships.

In the summer of 1987, I started a relationship with my first boyfriend. I was twenty-two years old and was teaching summer school in Salamanca, New York. My family believed Tom and I were just friends. I was still seeing Tom when I graduated from St. Bonaventure in May 1988 and moved back home with my parents. In July, Tom and I were having trouble. I was restless at home and ambled next door to my sister Maura's to try sorting things out in my mind. I sat at her picnic table and moped around her back yard teary-eyed until she came out to talk to me.

"What's wrong, Paul?" she asked, scooping back her dark bangs.

"It's Tom," I told her instantly. "We've been in a serious relationship for a year now, and things aren't going so great at the moment."

Although I hadn't come out to her, Maura didn't appear shocked to hear that we were a couple. She listened with a kind heart and offered gentle words of encouragement. "It's okay, Paul," she said. "I have gay friends. I love them, and I love you." She hugged me, and I was grateful to her, despite the fact that I had not resolved my problems with Tom. I was grateful at least to have the support of one of my family members. She later shared the news with her husband, who told me he was also supportive.

Tom and I worked through our differences and resumed our relationship. One night in late July, I decided to spend the night with him in the privacy of his apartment, as I had done several times already that summer. I called home to let my parents know.

My mother's voice was stern. "No, Paul. We want you home right now."

"Right now? But why? Is something the matter?"

"You are to come home right now."

I knew there was no point arguing. On the way home, I couldn't stop worrying. I wondered, *What do they know? Did someone tell them about Tom and me? How will I tell them?* In my anxiety-ridden state, I drove over the speed limit, but it seemed I couldn't get there quickly enough. I knew from Mom's tone that nothing bad had happened, no one was hurt. However, I got the feeling that she wasn't pleased and a lecture was in order.

It was late when I pulled into the driveway. The lights were on in the TV room where my parents spent their evenings. I walked in through the back door, and when I stepped into the TV room, I could tell by the cold look on their faces that a heated argument was in store.

"I don't understand. Why did I have to come home?"

They both glared at me. My mother shifted in her armchair. "It has been brought to our attention that Tom is gay," she said finally.

"Yes, I know," I said matter-of-factly. I took a breath. "And so am I."

I had wanted to tell them for so long, and as disappointed as I knew they would be, an incredible weight lifted from my body. I stood taller and returned their stony-eyed stares with a stiff smile. Their hurtful expressions brought back flashes of my most pained moments—all my fears and confusion, the endless, tearful prayers I had prayed, and how I had wanted to die rather than face the consequences of being "bad." I scowled at them, remembering those years, trying to convey the damage I had suffered in their overzealous household. I stood my ground.

It seemed as though five minutes of silence passed before my mom spoke. "We can get you some help," she said quietly.

I looked up at the ceiling, shook my head, closed my eyes. "I am fine with it, Mom. I don't need help." I tried to explain my feelings, how I loved Tom.

My mother burst into tears.

Dad leaned forward in his chair and stared at me hard through his glasses. "What you're feeling is just a crush, Paul. It's not love."

We talked for an hour without making any headway. My mother cried through much of the conversation. I felt bad, yet I saw in her a mirror image of myself, deeply sad and profoundly confused for so many years.

The next day began my official shunning. As the youngest in the family, I had witnessed my parents doing this to my brothers and sisters for their indiscretions. Over the next few weeks, I was limited in terms of use of the car, finances, and any show of affection. I felt like a stranger in my own home. My siblings grew distant, and I knew that they had been ordered to act that way as part of my punishment. At the dinner table, no one spoke to me. When I walked into a room, all conversation stopped. Literature on the wickedness of homosexuality was strewn about the house, appearing on the kitchen counter, in my bedroom, and everywhere else I went.

One day, Maura came over and asked me to go for a ride with her. I thought she might have wanted to tell me that she had been the one who had told our parents about Tom. When we arrived at Allen Park and she put the car in park and handed me a letter, I knew she had become a pawn for my parents.

"What's this?" I held the letter up and shook my head.

She turned and looked out the window. "Just read it."

I unfolded the paper and read the words that seemed to have been written in my sister's hand. The message was clear: being gay would result in me going to hell. Scripture was quoted. I knew she hadn't written that letter by herself, that it contained much of my parents' thoughts and beliefs. Maura was even quieter than I expected she would be, as if a sense of shame had come over her.

Although the letter made me angry, I managed to stay calm. I had suspected for some time that this would happen, that my sister would betray me.

I don't remember the drive home, but I remember knowing my life had changed forever. And as painful as it might have been, it had to be this way. I had to live authentically.

About a week later, my mother asked me to take her for a ride, and so I did. Rather than a letter, she had a lecture to offer me. She said she was concerned about my soul going to hell. She quoted scripture. I wondered whether she was concerned about my soul, or whether she was concerned over what people would say about me and how that would reflect on her.

A couple weeks later, in early August, my parents set up an appointment for us to meet with a counselor through the Diocese of Buffalo. By then I had already started to grow numb to their words. Because of their shunning and coldness toward me, I had detached myself from them. They had become toxic. I was in survival mode. However, I went willingly to counseling with them that day. I spent the ninety-minute ride to Buffalo in the back seat, occasionally tuning in to the noise of the radio or my parents' conversation, but mostly lost in my own thoughts about how I could escape their stranglehold, how I might break free from their fanatical following of the church.

After a brief wait in the counselor's office, a middle-aged gentleman came out and asked to speak with me alone.

In his office, he offered me a chair and took his place behind the desk. "Why are you here?"

"I'm gay, and my parents want me to change."

"Are you happy?"

"Yes," I told him. "Quite happy now. I feel liberated, as though I can live a true and purposeful life. But I'm not happy with my family's response."

He asked me to elaborate, and I told him about the shunning.

He seemed confounded. "I don't understand what the problem is."

After our discussion, which lasted about fifteen minutes, I waited in the lobby while my parents went in. Thirty minutes later, they hurried from the counselor's office, and I followed them out the door.

My parents were silent on the drive back. We never spoke of that day again, and I knew things would never be the same. The place we returned to would no longer be my home, and soon after that, I would move out of my parents' house. This would mark the beginning of a long and agonizing separation from my family—an estrangement that would span seven years.

***

The weekend after moving Tyler to the University of Cincinnati, we made the 100-mile trip to Berea College to see Tevin off. The college had sent Tevin a schedule of events for new student orientation that included family members, so we knew we'd be there for the day.

When we arrived that morning, traffic was thick but flowing steadily, thanks to signs posted all over campus directing us where to go. We followed the arrows to the front lawn outside the President's House. A crew of students swarmed our truck to get Tevin's bags and boxes and show us to Dana Hall, a four-story, red brick building in the middle of campus reserved for male freshmen. The campus itself was scenic and peaceful, with evidence all around of the college's heavy emphasis on environmental stewardship, including the garden, the greenhouse, the composting site, and recycling bins. We packed Tevin's belongings into the small dorm room, which had concrete block walls and a ceiling so low that you could reach up and touch it without stretching.

Randy ran his hands along the wood finish of one of the desks. "This is the same stuff they used when I was a student here," he said. "Students in the labor program build these pieces on campus."

I examined the bed frame and chairs a little more closely.

Tevin perked up slightly. I looked around, wondering if he would acclimate to sharing such a small room with a stranger.

When his roommate finally arrived, we noticed he was not wearing shoes, and his hair was somewhat disheveled. He introduced himself as Jordan. He and Tevin shook hands.

Jordan's parents and younger sister were in tow, all of them seemingly curious as to why these two white men were helping the black kid set up his room.

I smiled at his parents, "It's tough leaving our son, but we know it's going to be a great experience for him."

They nodded slowly, as though the reality of our situation was taking hold. The mother, a small sandy-haired woman, echoed my sentiments.

"I graduated from Berea and absolutely loved it here," Randy interjected.

"It's a lovely campus," the mother managed.

It was obvious that Jordan's family understood our situation, but they made no attempt to be friendly, and so we let the conversation die, giving them as much space as possible in the tiny dorm room while we figured out Tevin's itinerary for the remainder of the day.

Tevin himself was reserved and business-like the whole morning, perusing the schedule to figure out where we needed to be at what time. We went with him to get his student ID validated and make sure that his financial aid and other paperwork were squared away. Then the three of us ate lunch together in the cafeteria.

The afternoon seemed to drag by, perhaps because Randy and I were worried whether our son would be okay in this strange new environment. We kept casting each other nervous glances. Whereas Tyler had been happy and upbeat when we left him, Tevin was glum and hesitant about being at Berea. There had been no friends, nobody to dance with when he walked through the door. But Randy and I knew that it was more than just the lack of friends and the freshman jitters. Berea had not been Tevin's first choice—Northern Kentucky University had; Berea had been the most affordable option with free tuition through its work-study program. Tevin had been assigned to work as a carpenter for the school's theatre department, which seemed a good prospect considering his love of theatre, but the use of power tools and the manual labor required would end up making the assignment a bad match for him.

Besides that, I knew that Tevin, like me, was introverted and probably felt like an awkward urbanite among the mostly rural, Appalachian student population. He was sitting, quite intentionally, on the periphery of all the excitement, watching like a lonely outsider. He was disconnected.

Before the parting ceremony began, we tried to reassure him things would get better.

"It's different here, but you'll adjust," I told him.

"Just give it some time, Tev," Randy added. "You'll see."

In the courtyard, an official gave some welcoming remarks, then the college president addressed the crowd. There was a music presentation, and soon after that the "parting" process began, where an announcer read off students' names, and, one by one, they left their families' sides and sprinted over to the other side of the courtyard.

We knew Tevin's turn was coming. Randy and I took advantage of the extra time to hug him goodbye, each of us holding on a little longer than we normally did.

Tevin forced a smile and stepped back from us, jamming his hands in his pocket and looking out across the lawn in front of Phelps Stokes Chapel, where a new community awaited him—students, staff, and faculty representing the Berea family. He stood at attention waiting for his name to be called, and I admired his posture and his stature. He had grown taller than both Randy and me, and despite his self-consciousness, he looked strong and competent in a dark striped T-shirt and white shorts, his new student ID dangling from a lanyard on his neck.

"Tevin Johnson-Campion..."

When his name was called, he glanced our way briefly, a silent goodbye, and jogged across the lawn amid applause and cheering. We added as much noise as possible, calling after him, clapping and whistling to show our support. After high-fiving those who had already crossed over, Tevin took his place in line among the other students who had officially joined the Berea community.

Randy held onto my arm, as though he might collapse from sadness, and I could see he was fighting back tears. I hugged his shoulders and rubbed his back as we watched the rest of the ceremony. We were letting go of a miracle—the boys we had been given the honor to raise from birth. There was no easy way to do this. Our love for them was as deep as any parent's love.

17: Meeting the Press

Randy

It was a frosty February day. The sky had that washed-out winter look, the palest of blues with a thin skin of clouds muting the morning light. I was on special assignment at my company's Nashville office for the week, temporarily filling the quality manager's role while also, I suspected, being steered clear of my boss, Bill, who disliked me because I was gay. My career had come to a grinding halt six months earlier on that morning I'd revealed to Bill and another coworker that I had a male partner, and that his prostate-specific antigen level had been zero following a prostatectomy. It had been awkward trying to share my joy over Paul's successful treatment while my boss, an executive for a company that's supposed to celebrate health-care successes, turned up his nose to my news.

I was glad to have that distance from Bill, but I resented the time away from my family. I sat at my desk, hands poised over the keyboard, tracing the jagged corners and hard edges of the Nashville skyline with my eyes while my mind processed the previous day's incidents and scrambled for ways to improve cost-effectiveness and efficiency.

During a board meeting later that morning, I got a text message from Shannon Fauver, one of the attorneys working the same-sex marriage lawsuit we had joined against the state of Kentucky. Shannon's message read, "Anticipate Judge Heyburn's ruling to be announced at noon today. If in our favor, we will have press conference with plaintiffs this afternoon."

Heyburn's ruling? Press conference today? A moment of panic took hold, then elation. If Heyburn ruled that Kentucky had to recognize same-sex marriages performed in other jurisdictions, then Paul and I would be legally recognized as a married couple! Could this really be happening? Could it be true? I had hoped but never dreamed it imaginable. I sat stunned in the black leather high-back chair, elbows propped on the huge mahogany table, and stared at my phone, trying to decide my next move. I glanced at the time. It was almost ten AM. I excused myself from the meeting and returned to my office.

On instinct, I called Shannon instead of messaging her back.

"Hi Randy," she answered. "I knew you were working out of town, so I thought it might be best to give you a heads up." Shannon spoke hastily and her words were muddled. It took a minute for what she said to register.

"So, is this good news? Should I head back up to Louisville?" I asked eagerly.

Her short, sharp laughs sounded like happy barks. "I can't tell you what the ruling is, but you and Paul will certainly be happy about it. Technically I can't say anything until Heyburn releases his statement at noon, so…"

"Wow! It is good news," I blurted out, trying to keep my voice low. I got up from my desk and started pacing in front of the tinted glass windows, watching the door to make sure no one was standing there listening. "I guess I better cancel some meetings and drive home."

"Yes. Great idea," replied Shannon. "Having all the plaintiffs there will help put the right spin on the story."

"Where will it be?"

"Here at the office," she said. "At two o'clock."

I grabbed a pen from my desk and scribbled the info on a sticky note. "We'll see you there. Thanks, Shannon."

When I turned around, a coworker, Donna, was standing in the doorway with a folder tucked under one arm. "Hi, Randy. Have you read through those records yet?"

"Yes, I have, and I have a few things that need to be followed up," I answered, grabbing my suit jacket from a hook on the back of the door and tucking my phone and the sticky note into my pocket. I needed to call Paul, and I needed some privacy to do it. "But you know what? Something's come up, and I've got to head back to Louisville in about an hour. I need to step out for just a minute, but when I get back, can you help me reschedule some things?"

Donna noted my smile and took it as a cue that this was all business. "Sure. Just let me know who to call."

I thanked her and took the elevator to the parking garage, which was cold and empty except for the vehicles. I thought it would be a brief conversation, so I lingered near the elevator, pulled out my phone, and tapped the call icon next to Paul's name. He answered in a formal tone that let me know he was with someone.

"I know you're probably busy, but I just got some great news from Shannon."

"Really? What is it?" The subtlest note of cheer rang in his voice.

"Judge Heyburn's ruling," I told him. "He's announcing it at noon today. Shannon couldn't say anything officially, but it seems it's going to be in our favor."

"Oh, wow," Paul whispered. "That's fantastic."

"The thing is, they're holding a press conference this afternoon at two o'clock, so I'm canceling some meetings and heading back. The only reason Shannon let me know ahead of time is because she knew I'd have to drive from Nashville."

Paul was silent on the other end.

I shivered and shoved my free hand into my pocket for warmth. My fingers found the rumpled sticky note. I pulled it out and looked at it absently. "So I'll probably drive straight to their office for the press conference. Can you meet me there?"

He hesitated. I knew what was coming.

"I can't do it. I have an appointment this afternoon."

"What!" I snapped, wadding up the sticky note and squeezing it in my fist. "Are you kidding me?"

"I can't leave. I have a very important parent meeting this afternoon. We schedule these well in advance. I can't just cancel it at the last minute."

Despite the cold, I could feel the heat rising in my neck. "But we committed to this. We're part of the case. We knew these situations were going to happen. They need us to be there. We have to go!"

"No, we didn't sign up for me having to leave school at the drop of a hat." Paul did not raise his voice, but his words were firm and clear. "My first commitment is my work. It's too hard trying to reschedule parent meetings. It's hard enough to get parents to meet in the first place. A lot of them are working two jobs or have to make special arrangements for transportation."

I was too upset to see his side of things. "What about us? Where does our relationship factor in? Am I second to your job?"

"Of course not. But do you realize I'd have to use a family emergency as an excuse for leaving? I don't have any personal days left, and this hardly seems like a family emergency to me."

"That's bullshit," I grumbled. "I consider it an emergency. I'm driving three hours to be there, even if you refuse to show up." My hand was numb from holding the phone. I switched to the other hand. "I guess I'll just have to do this by myself."

I punched the end-call button without saying goodbye and marched back to the elevator, infuriated. On the ride up to the office, alone and exhausted from arguing, I closed my eyes and bowed my head. This was probably the most important breakthrough in our twenty-three-year relationship. How could he just blow it off like this?

Back at the office, Donna helped me contact the folks I was supposed to have meetings with that day and reschedule them for later in the week. I finished some work on a report, signed off on some paperwork, thanked Donna for her help, and walked out the door at eleven AM.

Traffic was typically light this time of day, but roadwork on Interstate 65 made getting out of Nashville slow and frustrating. I was already irritated. Now I would be pressed for time. Once I cleared the construction zone, I called Tevin, who was now attending the University of Louisville; he had only lasted a semester at Berea, unable to adjust to the rural environment. I was glad to have him back home.

When I told him about Heyburn's ruling, Tevin was his typical reserved yet excited self. "That's awesome. That's really, really big news."

His enthusiasm lifted my mood. "I know! Look, I mainly wanted to let you know in case you're interested in coming to the press conference. It's going to be at Dawn and Shannon's office on Frankfort Avenue at two o'clock."

"Yes," Tevin responded. "I'd really like to be there. I'll meet you guys there at two."

"Great!"

I tried to stay upbeat the rest of the drive home, but the landscape was dismal and depressing. The trees were bare and the ground had that hard, frozen look, as though nothing would ever grow out of it again.

To pass the time, I practiced a few talking points for the press conference. I wanted to say "It's a historic day for all Kentuckians that Judge Heyburn recognizes the significance of nontraditional families like ours." But I wasn't sure whether to say "a historic" or "an historic."

I repeated it both ways, listening to the sound of it, trying to decide which sounded better. I knew the rule that "a" precedes words that begin with consonants, but I also knew there were exceptions.

I was still upset about Paul. I waited until I crossed the state line into Kentucky to call him again. I knew that he would have already made up his mind by then, and I desperately hoped that he had broken down and used the family emergency excuse. I really did not want to go to this press conference by myself. I wondered whether any of the other plaintiffs would show up by themselves. I worried about giving the impression that Paul and I weren't a unified front.

When he answered the phone, I tried to sound cheerful. "Hi, Dad. Did you work things out so that you can meet me at the press conference?"

"Yes, I did." There was an edge in his voice. "We got hold of the parent, and it turned out she needed to reschedule our meeting today."

Already in my mind I was cheering, but I knew he wasn't finished, so I waited silently, with what must have been a big dopey grin on my face, steering with one hand and pumping my fist with the other.

"So I filled out the family emergency form and handed it in to the assistant principal." He paused. "I lied to be with you today. I love you, Randy Johnson."

18: A Family Emergency

Paul

Atriad of curious fifth-grade girls stared at me from their seats around the kidney-shaped table in the long, narrow space of my office. No matter my attempts to shield them from the conversation—lowering my voice and cupping my hand around the phone, moving to the far corner of the office—the girls understood I was speaking with someone about a serious topic.

After Randy hung up on me, I tried to be nonchalant as I put my phone away. One of the girls eyed me suspiciously, palms flat on the table, chin resting on laced fingers. Another squinted at me, arms folded across her chest. The third student chewed on the ends of her braids and smiled at me.

I smiled back and took my seat at the table. "Look, here's what I think we should do," I told the girls, and I laid out a plan to diffuse the alleged bullying. Under normal circumstances, I would have guided them through the process, urging them to brainstorm and come up with their own solution, which they would have been more likely to follow. I would have been careful to make sure no one left the conference with hurt feelings.

But today was different. I had a problem of my own to deal with. I had to lie to my boss, and it was a lie that I undoubtedly would be caught in—on camera. On live TV.

As I walked the three students back to their classes, I thought of the potential outcomes. Would I be able to justify using the family emergency excuse if anyone questioned it? I tried to bear in mind the greater good that would result, the freedom and acceptance that would be gained by the next generation of gays and lesbians, how much hardship might be circumvented as a result of Heyburn's ruling.

My first priority, however, was to try to reschedule the parent meeting I had scheduled for the afternoon. I asked the office clerk to contact the parents.

"No answer," she reported a few minutes later. "I left a message. I'll try back again in a few minutes."

I thanked her and retreated to my office to locate the form I needed to fill out. I sat at the kidney-shaped table trying to imagine my principal's reaction to seeing me on the news. *Maybe I shouldn't go through with it*, I thought, staring down at the form. It would be terrible for the parents to show up for our meeting only to be told I had to leave unexpectedly, and then for them to discover that my so-called emergency was a press conference on a gay marriage ruling. It was a risky proposition.

Just then, the office clerk popped into my office. "They completely forgot about the appointment today, and they want to reschedule."

It seemed too perfect to not have been Divine Providence. "Couldn't have worked out better," I responded.

Since the principal was in a meeting, I handed in the family emergency form to the assistant principal, who sat working at her desk. She looked up at me. "Is everything okay?"

"Yeah, everything's fine," I said, and that was all. I left her office promptly to avoid questions.

As I was organizing my room and preparing to leave, the on-site social worker stopped by. "Is your family okay, Paul? Is there anything I can do for you?"

"I'm fine. We're all fine," I told Chris, waving my hand dismissively in his direction. I met his eyes briefly, said, "Thank you," and returned to my work. I felt rude and underhanded for not revealing the truth to anyone—the truth being that the family emergency was a TV appearance. But another, deeper truth that troubled me was that I was terrified. I was terrified not only of my boss and coworkers discovering my "family emergency," but also of parents' reactions to my sexual orientation. I had suffered the prejudice of a parent as a public school teacher when Tevin and Tyler were babies. The memory of that incident pained me still.

***

Randy and I were living with his mother and stepfather in the tiny rural town of Belmont, where the local pastor preached against "niggers" and "queers" and Confederate flags flew freely from the beds of mud-flecked four-by-fours. I was teaching in Mount Washington, the most progressive municipality in the county, at Old Mill Elementary, one of the best schools in the district. It was springtime. The weather had warmed up, and families were getting outdoors for barbecues and ball games on weekends.

One sunny Saturday, Randy and I decided to make a trip to the local Walmart for diapers and summer outfits for the boys. The store was located in the northern part of the county, only a couple miles from the suburbs of Louisville and a more diverse world. We usually blended in easily there, although sometimes, when we spotted coworkers or parents, we would part ways, one of us ducking into the nearest aisle heading in the opposite direction. With my teaching job and Randy working as a nurse, we thought it best to avoid confrontations that might hurt our professional careers.

We arrived at the store early, ahead of the bigger crowds, and were walking the perimeter aisle between sporting goods and home furnishings when I spotted Marilyn, a bright-eyed fifth grader, skipping toward us, a few beats ahead of her mother. I was holding Tevin, walking alongside the cart that Randy was pushing while carrying Tyler. It was too late for me to veer off. Marilyn already held me in her line of vision, her grin widening. She was a sweet girl who'd had a hard time adjusting that year, although her attitude and grades had steadily improved. She waved at me and wheeled around, grasping her mother's arm and urging her forward.

At first, Mrs. Walker smiled at me, even after seeing that the baby in my arms was black. "Hi, Mr. Campion." She seemed slightly puzzled and pointed at Tevin, letting her finger fall away when she noticed Randy lingering behind me.

I took a step toward them. "Hello, Marilyn. Mrs. Walker. How are you?"

"Is that your baby?" Marilyn asked.

The mother's eyes darted between Randy and me. Her face fell.

"Yes, it is." I turned around so that Marilyn could see Tevin's face over my shoulder. I heard her giggle, but when I looked back, her mother was steering her away from me—away from us, Randy and me and the boys. She glared at me, her lip snarled in disgust, before stalking off, one arm draped protectively across Marilyn's back, ushering her ahead as quickly as possible.

Several weeks later, I returned to school. I had taken family leave following the twins' birth. The principal briefed me on a situation involving Mrs. Walker. "She came in demanding that her daughter be removed from your class," explained Helen Harrah, shaking her head. Helen had the thoughtful, gentle look of a librarian, with short cropped hair and neat, wire-rimmed glasses that framed her soft features. "When I asked why, she said because she didn't want her daughter getting AIDS from the teacher." She used her fingers to emphasize quotation marks around AIDS.

I recalled the way Marilyn's mother had glared at me in the store, the hateful look in her eyes, how she had bolted from the scene.

Helen leaned forward and raised an eyebrow. "So I used the opportunity to educate Mrs. Walker on how HIV is contracted—not through water fountains or drinking glasses, but by the exchange of bodily fluids," she said. "I pointed out that you are a respected teacher here and an esteemed colleague, and, of course, she had nothing negative to report in regards to your teaching."

I appreciated the principal's tact, yet I couldn't shake the shock of the mother's outrageous assumption. What hurt most was that Mrs. Walker had been kind and grateful to me in the middle of the school year. She'd even sent a Christmas card thanking me for working with Marilyn. I was disheartened by the fact that this same woman could have harbored such hatred in her heart. I thought of the boys and all the prejudice they were bound to face in the years ahead. I thought of Randy and the sadness and loneliness he'd felt as a child living in this place. I remembered the apologetic look on his face at the store when Mrs. Walker realized we were a couple. It was exhausting and painful to live this way. It was a wonder we had survived it.

***

This is why I was nervous the day of the press conference. I worried about parents' perception of the issue, their preconceptions, and the potential backlash. Although the world had changed in the nearly two decades since then, Kentucky was a red state with largely conservative leanings. There was bound to be an outcry from the religious right on the matter.

I was shutting down my computer and getting ready to leave when Randy called back. There was no trace of anger in his voice from our earlier conversation. Instead he sounded cheerful and upbeat, as though he'd just gotten word of Heyburn's ruling. We were the victors, after all. Our case had won. We should have been celebrating.

Randy wanted to know if I'd made arrangements to leave work.

My mood lifted as I told him what I had done. "Yes, I lied to be with you today," I said. But rather than feel remorse, I now saw this as a virtuous deed—a necessary act of defiance and a courageous show of love.

Although I convinced myself in that moment that I was justified in using the family emergency excuse, I had to fight to keep the feeling alive on the drive to Shannon and Dawn's office. Guilt kept creeping in. And nervousness. I hated being in front of the camera.

By the time I parked my car outside the law office, a bevy of text messages had hit my inbox, friends congratulating and thanking Randy and me for being part of the lawsuit. It seemed I hadn't fully understood the gravity of our role and how much it would mean to others. I was touched by the show of support and felt a burst of courage going forward.

Randy was waiting for me. We hugged each other, and Randy held onto my hand and pulled me close. "Look who just walked in the door," he said, and I turned around to see Michael Aldridge, the Kentucky ACLU director. He looked professional in red-framed Harry Potter-style glasses and a suit jacket.

While the media was assembling lights and camera, Dawn and Shannon corralled us to a corner of the room. We greeted the other plaintiffs with hugs and handshakes—Jim and Luke, Kim and Tammy, and Greg and Mike.

"Now we have to face the press," Dawn said. "Let's prepare for what might be asked today." She coached us individually and gave us encouraging feedback. "Each couple will be given the opportunity to speak. Think about what you're going to say. Repeat it in your mind. Say it aloud a few times." She made a twirling motion with her hands, as though urging us to open up.

More people arrived, including Chris Hartman, the head of the Kentucky Fairness Campaign, who was sporting his new Google Glass, a computer designed to be worn like eyeglasses that operated by voice command. He came over to congratulate all the plaintiffs. The room grew heady with excitement. When Tevin showed up, we proudly introduced him to Dawn and Shannon and the other plaintiffs, who took great interest in him, asking him questions about life at U of L and his career plans. For the next few minutes, we were all smiles and laughter, talking each other up and feeling good about the announcement. It felt like a party.

After consulting with the news representatives, Shannon motioned for us to gather on one side of the conference table facing the media, with those designated to speak sitting at the table and their spouses standing directly behind them. I stood behind Randy, and as the lights burned bright in our faces, I felt a warmth from within, a rush of gratitude that we had somehow made it to this day. I knew that Randy had practiced the lines, but when he said them, I had to swallow hard to keep myself from melting into a weepy mess. "This is a historic day for all Kentuckians. When discrimination exists, everyone suffers."

Luke sat next to us, and his words brought on the tears I'd managed to hold back when Randy spoke. "Jim and I have been together for forty-six years. This day means so much to us. We never thought it would come, not in our lifetime."

He related a story from his teenage years, when he had overheard his parents talking about him through the heating vent in his bedroom. His father's voice was stern. "What are we gonna do about that queer?" Luke said he had survived three suicide attempts. "It's not just about us today," he said. "It's for all those kids coming up behind us."

I remembered my youth and the secret cloak. The cloak of shame. My crush on Chachi from "Happy Days." My father's anger and my mother's tears. My incessant prayers, locked in the bathroom. The sleeping pills on the edge of the sink. My heart crying out.

I wondered how I had ever doubted that this was a family emergency.

19: Celebrating Strides

Randy

When I got back to Louisville, Paul and I decided to host a party at our house for the plaintiffs in the case.

"It would be a good way for all of us to get to know each other better, you know?" I stepped into the closet to hang up my suit.

Paul was already in bed tuning the TV via remote control. He paused and nodded. "That's actually a great idea." He was thinking now, his eyes focused on something far beyond the walls of our bedroom. "We really have no idea what happens from here—whether the state's going to appeal the decision or if they're going to go ahead and start letting gay and lesbian couples get their marriage licenses." He suddenly closed his eyes and whipped his head back and forth. "Is this really happening? I mean, gay marriage in Kentucky?"

I laughed and climbed into bed. "I know! Isn't it great?" I cuddled up next to him, slipping an arm around him and squeezing. "So how about next Saturday for the party?"

***

The day of the party was a flurry of activity. We decided not to fuss over the food to keep things simple. Tevin went after fruit and vegetable trays that we ordered from Paul's Fruit Market, and I drove over to Bootleg Bar-B-Q to pick up the main entrée and sides for our meal.

It was cool and cloudy that day, too cool to do anything outdoors. When I got home, I told Paul not to bother cleaning the deck area since it would be cold and close to dark by the time our guests arrived.

"One less thing to worry about," he said, and helped me haul the food in from the garage.

Shannon and her daughters, Soha and Tayma, were the first to arrive. We showed them in and offered them drinks. Kenzie invited the girls to sit in the living room while Paul and I made small talk with Shannon in the kitchen.

Our conversation hadn't gone far when Greg and Mike showed up with their teenagers, Bella and Isaiah. Paul and I had met Greg and Mike at a gay and lesbian parenting group in Louisville years earlier and had maintained a steady friendship with them since then. Because they had been involved in the Kentucky lawsuit early on, the case had been filed under Greg's last name and was thus called *Bourke v. Beshear*.

Tevin and DeSean greeted Bella and Isaiah, and the kids ambled around the house, eventually retreating to the home theater in our basement.

Soon after that, Dawn appeared with a bottle of Early Times and a wide grin. She hugged me, Paul, and everyone else, then got in the food line that was now snaking through the kitchen.

Kim, Tammy, Luke, and Jim were the last to arrive, the couples we knew the least about.

Paul and I were the youngest of the bunch. I was eager to learn more about the other plaintiffs. I knew that we were all stronger as a unit, much in the same way I had felt after meeting Paul that fateful night in August 1991. It didn't matter that I'd never come out as gay, that I'd grown up in a church and a community that considered homosexuality an abomination to God. What mattered was that I had fallen in love, and I somehow knew that the power of our togetherness would defeat the hate and the ire we faced in the days ahead. As clichéd as it might have sounded, there was strength in numbers. That truth was punctuated by the legal case we had just won, along with these three other couples, all with stories of hardship and heartache that they had faced as a result of discrimination.

We dug into the barbeque and found spots to sit and eat. I made sure Kim and Tammy had everything they needed. Kim had a finely lined face with bright blue eyes and short hair. Tammy looked impossibly younger than she could have been, since she and Kim had been high school friends. Her skin was smooth, and her dark, shoulder length hair was lightly streaked with gray. They were a sweet couple, happy simply to be together.

After dinner, we congregated in the basement and shared our hopes and dreams for the outcome of the case. Greg and Mike sat on one end of the sectional sofa, Luke and Jim on the other. Greg, who was slim and clean-cut with graying hair, posed the question we all wanted to know: "What happens if the governor appeals Heyburn's decision?"

Shannon tilted her head appreciatively, as if to say she hoped this would not be the case. "Then we wait," she said. "They will have to put together a case, and the case then has to be heard by the Sixth Circuit Court of Appeals."

Luke, a stout, vocal man with short gray hair and a rosy complexion, leaned forward. "So, say the state goes for the appeal. How long will it take for that to be heard?" He clasped Jim's hand and frowned. "We're not going to be around much longer, and we'd like to see this thing through. Get it settled once and for all."

Jim patted his hand. He was a calming figure with thinning, dusty brown hair and round eyeglasses that sometimes slid down the bridge of his slender Roman nose. He adjusted them quickly and directed his attention to the attorneys.

Dawn looked at Shannon and shrugged.

"There's no telling," Shannon said. "It could take months."

Luke was visibly distressed.

Although they were not as old as Luke and Jim, Mike and Greg were nearing retirement age. As a consequence, they were dealing with discriminatory issues regarding health-care decisions and retirement benefits. I knew these were matters that Paul and I needed to stay abreast of, that we would one day face ourselves—that we had already dealt with to some degree when Paul was diagnosed with prostate cancer. The question of parenthood also hung over them. Like us, only one of them could be the official parent of their children. Paul and I understood all too well the clashes and calamities that arrangement entailed.

Dawn looked around and sighed at the sight of us, slumped and deflated, as though the case were lost already. "We're going to get through this," she said. "Don't be so glum. Besides," she sidled up next to Shannon and nudged her with her elbow, "we have some good news to share, don't we?"

"That's right," said Shannon, raising her glass. "We have been approached by three other attorneys right here in Louisville who are willing to help with the case if the governor decides to appeal."

Kim let out a triumphant "Hooray!" and Tammy clapped enthusiastically. Jim and Luke muttered their approval.

"That's the good news," Shannon said. "The not-so-good news is that we do expect Beshear to file an appeal. He has an obligation to his constituents, and no matter how blatantly unconstitutional the gay marriage ban is, the people of Kentucky voted for it."

The room resounded with grunts and groans, even though we knew Heyburn had stayed his decision for a reason.

"We're going to need these other attorneys. They'll be a big asset to our case. They bring a different mix of skills and experience to the courtroom. We'll be happy to have them join us."

"What about attorney fees?" Greg asked. "How are we going to pay all of you for your time and trouble?"

We all perked up to hear Shannon's response. "That's a good question. You don't owe us a thing. We get paid when and if the case wins by the entities that have blocked your constitutional right to marry. That's the way the lawsuit works. All you will we be held accountable for are the filing fees associated with the case, as we discussed before."

Despite the relief we felt with that financial burden lifted, the mood had darkened, and we searched each other's faces for comfort.

Dawn piped up. "Look, y'all," she said, perching on the armrest of the couch. "We wouldn't be working this case if we didn't think we could win it." She shook her head and folded her arms across her chest. "We should be celebrating. We just won, and, yes, already they're throwing up a roadblock. So now we probably have to fight an appellate court. But we're going to win there, too!"

Some of us laughed, and some of us cheered. Her little speech was exactly what we needed to hear. Our spirits lifted, and conversations resumed.

I tried my best to believe Dawn's words. The battle was not over yet, but maybe the toughest parts had been fought. Maybe we had suffered the hardest hurts. I prayed to God that that was the case. I pleaded with God. *What now?* And some scripture came to me, from the Old Testament. *Be strong in the Lord. Put on the whole armor of God. The belt of truth. The helmet of salvation. The shield of faith.*

Paul was mingling with Kim and Tammy. He shot me a smile. As I moved toward him, I saw that his eyes were clear and his armor intact. The room brightened, and suddenly I was filled with hope.

20: Getting Some Distance

Randy

At the hospital where I worked in Louisville, we had added some criteria to our patient screening process to try to catch certain cancer diagnoses earlier. I was reviewing the results of those efforts when one of my employees knocked on the door outside my office, which stood open.

Monica leaned in, gripping the doorway with one hand and waving at me with the other. "You busy?" she asked.

"I've got some time." I rolled back from my computer and scooted to the open side of my desk. "What's up?"

Monica shut my office door behind her and slid into the seat facing me. "I got pulled into a meeting with Bill this morning to discuss all of our quality initiatives," she said, raising an eyebrow at me.

I got her drift instantly but played devil's advocate to eliminate any doubt. "I guess I'll get filled in later." I shrugged.

Monica smirked. "He told me I needed to report everything directly to him from now on. He called it a 'mentoring relationship'."

I squinted. "Is that right?"

She nodded, watching me. Monica had been a close confidant as well as a trusted colleague. In my office that day, her empathy showed. She was wringing her hands in her lap like an anxious mother.

I straightened the corners of some paperwork in a slot on the corner of my desk and rubbed my neck. This wasn't the first time Bill had usurped my authority. After six years in my leadership role, I had learned just recently that I had been left out of the loop on important new strategies, and that my name had been removed from the leadership team's email list. Ever since I had revealed, on that business trip in Nashville, that Paul was my partner, Bill had avoided me, revamping the reporting structure of our department so that he never had to meet with me and handing over my duties to other employees seemingly to eliminate the need for my position.

"I appreciate you letting me know," I told Monica.

She let out a long sigh, her body wilting as she stood to go. "Let me know if you need anything."

***

Later that day when I confronted Bill in his office, he sat stiffly at his desk with his chin tucked, steely eyes peering out from under the heavy brow bar of his trendy frames. He had a look of boredom on his face, as though offended that I would bring up such trivial matters. "I have my own ideas about restructuring and reorganizing your department," he said.

"But you never laid out a plan explaining exactly what you were doing and how all of this—" I spun my hands in the air, waiting for the right word—"all of these changes would improve our efficiency."

Bill stood up and walked around the desk, wearing the same expression as a temperamental sixth-grade boy, nostrils flaring, jaw jutting out, head tilted back as though prepared to dodge a swing. And at that moment I wanted nothing more than to drill him as hard and as fast as I possibly could. I could feel the heat rising in my neck, my respiration increasing. I stood taller and straighter, my eyes locked on his as he approached me.

"Listen here, Johnson." His voice and scowl seemed to soften at the last minute, but his beady, bloodshot eyes were hard as diamonds. "I don't have to explain anything to you. Get it? I'm the boss, and what I say goes."

I knew that I had to back down, that regardless of what I said, the matter would not be resolved.

So I said nothing. I refused to acknowledge his words and instead stood there waiting to gain my composure, resisting the urge to run from the room, which was, I kept telling myself, exactly what this bully wanted.

Bill gave me a mock look of pity and stepped back, folding his arms across his chest and clearing his throat. "Your job responsibilities no longer include management of the leadership team. Your job responsibilities no longer include working alongside the acting director, which is me. There are emails you will not be privy to anymore. That's none of your concern now. The strategies we develop are none of your concern now. That's just the way it's going to be, Johnson. Do I make myself perfectly clear?"

"You certainly do," I muttered through gritted teeth, and I spun on my heels and left before saying or doing something I might regret later.

***

When the corporate office contacted me a few weeks later about a special assignment in Atlanta, I practically jumped at the opportunity, not only to get out from under a bigoted boss, but also to take on a role that would give me more experience in executive leadership.

Paul and I discussed the decision in bed one night with the TV on mute.

"I know it'll be hard with everything we've got going on," I said. I worried about Paul juggling all the responsibilities of the kids and our household.

But he only shook his head and said, "No, you need this, Dad." He knew all about Bill—how he had treated me, how he had marginalized my role in the company. "It's a chance to get away from the miserable place you're in right now."

I could not deny how I'd grown to hate my job, how I despised getting in the car and driving to work every morning. On top of that, I felt guilty working Paul overtime to counsel me on it. "I love you so much," I said, and I hugged him against me.

I made plans to commute that summer, flying or driving home on weekends, with Paul making an occasional trip down to Atlanta. The company provided me a small, furnished hotel suite across the street from the building where I worked. I settled in as best I could, stocking up on drinks and snacks from the local Publix grocery to save time and money. I called Paul every morning before heading to the office and again every night before turning in. I slept on the right side of the bed, just as I did at home, and put the extra pillows long ways next to me on the left. Sometimes I woke in the morning clutching them, and was always sad when I realized I was alone in a hotel 400 miles from home.

That summer I worked closely with Betty, the chief nursing officer for the region, which encompassed eight hospitals spread over several states in the Southeast. Betty was a pretty lady in her late forties, tall and slender, with red hair and a bright smile. We spent a good deal of time with an executive team crafting a governance structure for all the hospitals to follow. Outside of that, Betty and I worked alongside each other on quality initiatives. We got along well and our time together was productive. During my stint, we discussed ways to improve patient care.

"What do you think about structuring a reporting process for hospitals to use so that we can track improvements in access to care?" she asked.

"I think that's a great idea," I replied, and I suggested measuring the blocks of time between patients signing in and seeing a health-care provider, and again between seeing a health-care provider and either being discharged or admitted for treatment.

Together we brainstormed reasons that would cause long wait times for patients.

"Saturation would be the number one reason," Betty suggested. "Sometimes, if only one or two doctors are on duty, then patients might have a two- to three-hour wait."

I jotted some notes and tried to keep in mind the high cost of low doctor-patient ratios.

Betty continued, as though reading my mind. "So if we determine patients should wait no longer than, say, an hour, then we would have to develop a contingency plan for calling in more providers to see more patients more quickly. And that could get expensive."

"Right," I said. "So the trick is going to be standardizing wait times in the most cost-efficient way possible."

We knew we needed real data for the next step. Betty volunteered to mine the company's database for numbers.

It was only Thursday morning, but already my thoughts had shifted to Friday. I wondered how the kids were doing and whether Paul had heard anything more from the attorneys about the same-sex marriage lawsuit. By now we knew that the governor of Kentucky was appealing Heyburn's decision, and that our attorneys would have to present oral arguments for our case to the Sixth Circuit Court of Appeals. In a surprising turn of events, Kentucky Attorney General Jack Conway had refused to fight the ruling, and so Governor Beshear had hired outside counsel to pursue the appeal.

Betty was seated in front of a desktop computer waiting for the database to respond. "Going home this weekend?"

"Actually, Paul's coming here," I told her, and the mere thought of seeing him brought a smile to my face.

She grinned at me. "How nice. You get a break from traveling, too." Unlike Bill, Betty was completely comfortable with my gay partner.

I told her about the sights we hoped to see—Centennial Park and a restaurant owned by one of Paul's old friends from Jamestown.

"You two should go to Stone Mountain," she said. "It's a great place to get outdoors. They have hiking trails and golfing and fishing. There's an old grist mill and a covered bridge. They have restaurants and shops, too. All kinds of stuff."

I thanked her. "Maybe we'll check it out."

Soon the database that we needed was up and running, and Betty redirected her attention to the computer screen. She pointed to a chair and made room for me. I pulled up a seat next to her, and together we started entering the parameters for the reports we needed to generate.

***

The day Paul and I trekked up Stone Mountain was hot and humid. It was a one-mile hike to the top of the unusual dome-shaped geological structure, which rose up like a giant bare rock from the fields and forests surrounding Atlanta. We knew little about the sight until we got there, and the more we discovered about the history of the place, the more unpleasant our experience became.

We were dressed in shorts and T-shirts, each of us carrying a bottle of water to stay hydrated. The trail was relatively busy that day, and we initially walked along the stone surface with great interest, marveling at the strange formation. Paul read somewhere that the mountain was actually a pluton formed from an outpouring of magma from the earth's crust that never made it to the surface. We also learned that there was a Confederate Memorial at the park, the world's largest bas-relief sculpture on the mountain's north face depicting Robert E. Lee, Stonewall Jackson, and Jefferson Davis. From a quick search on our phones, we found out that the site was where the second Ku Klux Klan formed in 1915.

"Creepy," I said, as we started up the trail.

Between scrolling our phones and reading historic markers along the way, Paul asked me how work was going. I filled him in on the projects I was involved in.

"I feel like I'm contributing something of value to the organization again. I feel good about what we're doing." Saying this out loud was like acknowledging it for the first time. I wiped my forehead with the back of my hand and readjusted my ball cap.

"Good," said Paul, patting my back as much a gesture of praise and affection as a way to encourage me along the trail, which was much steeper now.

Soon I was out of breath and drenched with sweat. We had to move to the side to allow the locals to pass us, many of whom apparently used the trail as an exercise course, hauling small bags of sand on their shoulders as they ascended the mountain.

Although the sun was not particularly bright that day, my body felt as though it was melting in the muggy heat. I felt exhausted. "Paul, I need a break. Just for a few minutes. I have to rest."

We found a spot off the trail where we could sit, practically collapsing into place. I held my head in my hands for a few minutes and breathed deeply, inhaling through my nose, exhaling through my mouth.

Paul squatted next to me. "Are you okay?"

I lifted my head. "I don't know. I might be dying. I'll let you know."

"That's not funny. Should I call for help?"

"No, I'll be fine."

Paul twisted the cap off a water bottle and handed it to me. "Drink it," he ordered, although rather mildly, like a parent commanding a sick child to take his medicine. Still, his assertiveness was a turn-on, and I grabbed hold of the flimsy plastic container and chugged the water obediently, winking playfully at him when I was done.

Paul rolled his eyes and tried to hide his smile. "Better?"

"I think so."

He helped me up.

It turned out that the worst part of the trail was behind us. Ten minutes later, we had scaled to the top, which seemed to me what it must be like to walk on the surface of the moon. There was no soil, no plant life at all, just a barren landscape of lumpy terrain and some rock pools.

The panoramic view that Betty and the park's brochure had touted was a disappointing backdrop to the haze and pollution that clouded the Atlanta skyline and neighboring countryside. If there was anything beautiful to behold, neither Paul nor I could see it. Perhaps our vision was spoiled by the fact that we couldn't see past the sorry history of the place, the remnants of racists and bigots that pervaded our lives to this day.

I searched the faces of the other visitors—the many white families and their children exploring the mountain floor. I looked for the lesbian couples and the tattooed grandparents, the bikers and the bible beaters. I wondered what it would take to live peacefully together in this world, to end the persecution once and for all.

I thought of Bill back in Louisville, enjoying the comforts of home and family, climbing into bed at night with his spouse. I felt resentment building inside me, like hot magma at the center of the earth. Here I was burning up on top of a memorial to a Confederacy that clung to racial oppression, in a sort of figurative hell, if not a literal one, with a river of fire below me. And somewhere in Kentucky, a homophobic boss was quietly taking over a department I had spent six years working to improve.

I had helped raise a wonderful, multiracial family under the most daunting circumstances, and my passion in that regard had spilled over into my work life, where I had strived to instill compassion and caring in a quality operation responsible for treating the weakest and the sickest among us. How someone like Bill could ever be effective in that position was beyond me. How would he feel about treating homosexual patients? I wondered. What if his own son was gay?

That night, I dreamed we were trudging up the trail at Stone Mountain—Paul and I, and Tevin, Tyler, Mackenzie, and DeSean. The struggle was real. I felt it in every bone in my body. I stopped to mop the kids' foreheads with an old rag that turned out to be a Confederate flag. The heat hurt our hearts. The sun blistered our skin. We slowed our pace. Even Paul had trouble keeping up. People kept pushing us aside on the trail, nearly trampling over top of us. We kept going because we knew something great awaited us at the top. As we got closer, we cried out for joy. We were soaked in tears and sweat, clasping hands, holding on to each other, holding out hope for whatever reward we would find there. Nirvana. Bliss. A world without prejudice. A higher love. God's love shining down on us. A voice booming, "Well done."

But there was nothing at the top of that mountain. Nothing but a rock floor and a hazy sky and the blank faces of so many sheep we had followed to get there.

21: Family, Food, and Gratitude

Randy

I was bitter about Kentucky Governor Steve Beshear appealing Heyburn's decision, even though our attorneys had everything worked out, even though they were optimistic about us winning the case. A motion to intervene filed by four new plaintiffs had bolstered our lawsuit; Tim Love and Larry Ysunza, and Maurice Blanchard and Dominique James had attempted to marry right after Heyburn's ruling and were denied marriage licenses. Over the summer, in *Love v. Beshear*, Judge Heyburn ruled in favor of the two couples seeking the freedom to marry, and the plaintiffs then became part of our case, too.

Our legal team grew, as well, adding Dan Cannon, Joe Dunman, and Laura Landenwich, three trial lawyers who brought new energy and oratory skills to the case. On August 6, 2014, Laura made the oral argument for *Bourke v. Beshear* before the Sixth Circuit Court of Appeals in Cincinnati.

I was still in Atlanta on special assignment, and I watched coverage that day on my desktop computer at work. Paul and I had been unable to make the trip to Cincinnati, but some of the other plaintiffs had gone. They sent Paul and me "wish you were here" messages and posted photos on Facebook of the rally they took part in outside the courtroom. After the rally, they crowded inside with the attorneys, Mike and Greg bringing along their teenage son and daughter for the historic occasion. Luke and Jim were there, and Kim and Tammy. I smiled at their pictures and longed to be there with them. I felt disconnected viewing it all on a screen, although as I scrolled through the coverage, I was proud of the plaintiffs who were there on our behalf, and I was encouraged by Laura's words.

"Kentucky's laws place a badge of inferiority on people and families, and it invades the sphere of individual rights protected by the Constitution," she argued. "The fundamental right to marry has not changed: What has changed is our understanding of what it means to be gay and lesbian. And now we must recognize that these individuals are entitled to the equal protection of the law and they are entitled to exercise their fundamental right.... The path to marriage equality has been laid. We now ask this court to walk down it."

I wanted to stand up in my office and cheer. I was still pissed off at Beshear for pursuing the appeal, especially in light of the fact that he'd had to hire outside counsel because Kentucky's attorney general, Jack Conway, had refused to be part of it. I just wanted the case to be decided, once and for all, and for Paul and I to be able to get on with our lives without the daily obstacles that troubled us as a gay couple with children.

But that day, my sour mood turned to sweet anticipation. The attorneys said we should brace for another blow, but that we shouldn't lose hope. Blogs on the Freedom to Marry and ACLU websites were speculating about our case, and other marriage equality cases, rising up through the system. There was talk that the matter might go all the way to the Supreme Court. In the weeks that followed, while we awaited the decision of the Sixth Circuit, the air bristled with excitement, sustaining me for the remainder of my time in Atlanta.

I returned home to Louisville with the feeling that something had changed, had shifted—regardless of the outcome of the appeal. When I hugged the kids, I remembered holding them in my arms as babies, and the joy on Paul's face back then, and the way my heart fluttered when I took in the sight of my beautiful family. I remembered DeSean as the small shell of a boy who had come to us seven years ago, now practically a grown man, as strong in spirit as he was in the flesh, and how much happiness he had added to our lives. I was hopeful then, and I was grateful.

***

"We lost." That was all Shannon's text message said when the Sixth Circuit Court of Appeals announced its decision in November.

Even before getting the message, I knew. We had all known. It was no surprise—the Sixth Circuit was infamous for overturning lower courts' rulings. It was simply the next step. We would appeal to the Supreme Court. If they agreed to hear our case, we would not only be fighting Kentucky's marriage ban, but representing the right to marry for all same-sex couples nationwide.

It was an exciting proposition, and over the next couple weeks, Paul and I talked incessantly about how fast everything had happened and wondered aloud about our chances of becoming a Supreme Court case. We talked to the other plaintiffs, and all of us bombarded the attorneys with questions. When would we know something? And if they agreed to hear the case, how long after that until the case was heard? What happened if they refused to hear it? They responded the best they could via group messages, and they shared links with us to relevant news and information regarding marriage equality cases nationwide. We knew there were several other lawsuits like ours that were being considered at the federal level, but we had no idea whether those cases affected ours or vice versa.

With the chaos of the year behind us, Paul and I looked forward to celebrating Thanksgiving with the kids and my extended family. We had hosted a potluck-style dinner at our house for the past decade. My sisters and brothers came, along with their sons and daughters, and everyone brought a dish or dessert. Violet made the dumplings. Brian fixed crock-pot green beans. Myrtle made sweet potato pie.

My brother Jim was the first to arrive, as usual. He parked his pickup on the street and hobbled up the sidewalk carrying a whole ham in a glass pan covered with aluminum foil. Jim was shorter than I was and nineteen years older, with graying hair.

I opened the door to greet him while Paul put our dog, Max, in his crate in the bedroom.

"Hey little brother." How's it going?" Jim said, stepping inside.

"Good. Come on in. How've you been?" I led him to the kitchen.

"Same as always," said Jim, setting the ham on the counter. "Good to see ya, Randy." He clapped me on the shoulder. "How are those kids? Whizzing through college now?"

"Yep. Tevin's still at U of L, and Tyler's in his second year at the conservatory. They're all here. Upstairs." I hitched a thumb at the ceiling. "Probably Snapchatting or Skyping. They'll be down in a bit. Is Julie still coming?" Julie was Jim's daughter.

"Oh yeah, she'll be here shortly, I expect."

I got out the cold cuts, which was our holdover food until everyone arrived. Jim fixed himself a plate and retreated to the living room to watch football. I was disappointed that he didn't mention anything about the marriage lawsuit. I tried to brush it off, but it was impossible to ignore. We had been all over the news. Our case had been heard in federal court. We were likely going to the Supreme Court. It was a very big deal. How could he ignore it? I wondered. Why would he ignore it?

My niece Tina, a red-haired, freckled beauty, arrived next with a broccoli casserole and her ten-year-old daughter, Sydney. Kenzie rushed down the steps and lured Sydney to the basement to watch TV in our home movie theater.

Tina and I chatted about the rest of the family. "Dad and Pam are on their way," she told me as I arranged some items on the counter. Paul was busy basting the turkey and peeling potatoes; the mashed potatoes and turkey were our contribution to the meal.

Soon the others arrived: Nicki, Brian, Violet, Myrtle; my brother Willie and his wife, Pam; my brother Bobby and his wife, Paula. The house filled with the cacophony of conversation, although none of the talk was about the historic case that Paul and I were involved in.

"Who else is getting up early to go shopping?" Nicki wanted to know.

"Not me!" Violet chimed in. "I would never fight those crowds."

"Me either." My niece, Kelly, stood at the stove dropping squares of dough into boiling water. "It's not worth getting trampled on."

"I get all my shopping done that day, and for half the money," Nicki said. "I love it."

Meanwhile, some of the kids were skimming sales ads, circling the gadgets and toys they wanted for Christmas. Tevin, Tyler, Tina, and Julie were congregated in the living room eating snacks and laughing at YouTube videos. The men were sprawled out on the couch watching the football game. Bobby's family had gathered in the dining room and were chatting about hunting season.

I handed out beer and made myself a drink, all the while fuming over the fact that no one had mentioned anything about the lawsuit. Paul headed me off on the basement stairs.

"Don't make an issue of it," he advised me. "Let's just have dinner and forget about it for the evening."

"I don't understand them," I said. "They're supposed to be my family. We're supposed to support each other. I thought they loved me. I thought they supported us!" I couldn't help feeling emotional.

Paul shook his head. "It's not worth ruining a holiday meal."

I gritted my teeth and stomped up the steps, determined to inflict guilt on my brothers. I would stare hard into their eyes, I told myself. No, I decided. I would say nothing. I wouldn't even smile. Then they would know how insulted I felt. They had to know what was going on. They saw my Facebook posts. They watched the news. Violet and Myrtle knew. I knew my sisters were afraid to bring up the matter in front of my brothers, and as strong as our bonds were and as deep as our love for each other was, I resented that. I recalled coming out to Bobby and how he had responded, as though my sexuality was like a death sentence for him.

"What are my friends going to think about this—about me, having a gay brother?" I remembered the look on his face, how he had smiled to lighten the blow. But he meant those words, no matter how agonizing they were to me, no matter how arrogant they sounded. I knew then that any relationship I would have with him in the future would be superficial, the way Paul's relationships with some of his family had turned out to be.

All this time I had thought my brothers supported me and wanted equality for me and Paul, but in truth they only tolerated my sexuality and my relationship with Paul. There were conditions when it came to matters of love. In essence, with their silence, my brothers told me, "I love you, but I don't agree with this part of your life, especially you being public about it."

My head thumped and my heart ached from the rejection. Suddenly, I was twelve years old again, and nothing would ease the pain of the truth—that I was attracted to other guys, that I pined for another guy's kiss, another guy's touch—his soul, his affections.

Before leaving, Violet, Myrtle, Paula, and my nieces helped put away leftovers and load the dishwasher. After everyone was gone, Paul and I sliced some Italian cream cake and collapsed onto the couch. The kids had retreated to their quarters upstairs. After we finished our dessert, we moved into the bedroom to debrief about the evening's outcomes.

"It really pisses me off," I said.

"I know," Paul replied. "But you have to understand that they're just not informed. Talking about homosexuality, about gay marriage ... that's totally out of their comfort zone."

"That's just ignorant," I said. "How could they refuse to see this for what it is? It's huge. It's history! How could they refuse to recognize any of our sacrifice or struggle all these years? They know what we've been through."

"Because they're concerned about their religious beliefs," Paul said, shrugging.

I knew he was right, but I hated to admit it. I hated to think my brothers had been so easily manipulated into believing that old school religious zealot stuff about homosexuality being an abomination to God.

"Maybe they don't understand the significance of the case. Maybe that's why they're not bringing it up," Paul offered.

I nuzzled up next to him and kissed his cheek. "I love you, Paul Campion."

"Love you, too," he responded, and burrowed into the blankets.

That night, I dreamed I was on trial, that I had taken the stand. I swore on the bible. The judge was a dark-haired lady with a Magic 8-Ball. The jury was my brothers. They stared at me, with eyes and hearts as hard as stone.

22: Parental Rights to a Rite of Passage

Paul

After nearly twenty years of parenting together, Randy and I thought we knew everything there was to know about hoop-jumping. By the time DeSean turned sixteen, we had grown used to finagling not only the usual bureaucracy involved in raising children, but also dealing with the added stress of a system that discriminated against homosexual couples. Because we were gay, we'd had to go through single-parent adoptions with each of our four children. Because we weren't jointly recognized as parents—at least not on paper—we'd had to grapple individually with medical bills, insurance paperwork, and government documents. As much as we wanted to function like a normal family, we simply couldn't when it came to official parent-child business, such as applying for a Social Security card. This became the latest hoop—an extra hoop—that we had to leap through to help DeSean get his driver's permit.

When we realized he would need a new card to apply for his permit, Randy volunteered to take him. "It's easier for me," he reasoned. "You'd have to take a vacation day. I can make up the hours." It was a relief to me. I was grateful we had such an efficient partnership when it came to our family.

The next day, Randy and DeSean sat for two hours in the cramped waiting area of the Social Security Administration office before they were called to a window. The customer service worker took DeSean's birth certificate and started the application process, typing data onto a computer. She asked Randy for his ID, and when he gave her his license, she frowned. "This doesn't match up," she said, pointing to the name on DeSean's birth certificate, where I was identified as the legal guardian, and the name on Randy's license.

"We're a couple," Randy tried to explain. "Paul Campion is my partner. DeSean is our son." He put a hand on DeSean's back.

"I'm sorry, sir. I completely understand the situation, but our hands are tied. We can't process the application without your partner's presence and signature."

Randy said she seemed genuinely sorry, but he was upset about the long wait, all for nothing. He said DeSean was quiet until they got in the car, at which point he turned to Randy and said, "That's why you guys need to be able to get married."

DeSean was patient over the ensuing weeks waiting for my holiday break to start so that we could go to the Social Security Administration and apply again. He knew that once we applied, he would have to wait another couple weeks to receive the card in the mail. Only then would he be able to take the written test for his driver's permit. He shrugged it all off, while Randy and I groaned about the inconvenience and the amount of time he was losing without the permit and, thus, his driver's license.

A few days before Christmas, we went to apply. I was nervous about the process and kept asking Randy, "Are you sure all I need is his birth certificate and my ID?" I was worried that the hoop would shrink or even worse catch fire.

Once we got there, we only waited half an hour to see a customer service representative. DeSean and I sat in a pair of chairs facing the window and watched as the worker tapped his computer keyboard over and over, glaring at the screen and shaking his head.

"There are so many discrepancies here," he explained. "I have to try to clear them out."

I nodded, as though I understood, but I didn't. My nervousness heightened. I recalled the little dogs that were forced to jump through flaming hoops at the Shrine Circus, and I briefly thought I knew the level of anxiety they must experience in the moment before springing off their paws into that dreaded ring of fire.

At one point, the worker called his supervisor over, and my stomach knotted up while they tried one solution after another for several minutes. Then, at last, they both uttered a small sigh-like cry of triumph, the kind of sound that a fan makes when his team finally scores in a particularly tense game. I felt a surge of relief. The circus dogs could go home now. Christmas was saved!

In January, after the card came in the mail, I had to get special permission to leave work early to take DeSean to the Department of Motor Vehicles. I didn't want to risk another debacle by sending Randy alone, but since he had the more flexible schedule, he picked up DeSean from school and the three of us met at the DMV.

I'd already taken a place in line and got so close to the front before Randy and DeSean arrived that I had to let someone go in front of me. It was a busy office, the main location in Louisville for permits and licensing. There were probably a hundred people there that day, most of them parents with their teenage sons and daughters. As we walked along the queue barriers, the typical kind of exchanges were taking place between parents and their sixteen-year-olds: unsolicited advice was either silently accepted with a blink and a nod or mocked with eye-rolls and crossed arms. The phrase, "I know, Mom," echoed in my ears for the next hour.

"I'm stepping out to make a few phone calls." Randy motioned to the door.

I saluted him.

DeSean sank back into his quiet demeanor. He seemed excited and a bit edgy, shifting and turning, finding nowhere to comfortably rest his coal-black eyes, which caught a lot of attention these days. He was a handsome lad with features that seemed more Greek in nature than his true African-American heritage. He had an angular face with a strong jaw that resembled Henry Cavill, and a faint mustache that topped off his grown-up look.

"How was your day at school?" I asked.

He shrugged. "Okay, I guess."

Suddenly his eyes were drawn to a girl in short furry boots and a hippie beanie whom he recognized from the Brown School. She waved happily and hurried over to the barricade. They chatted for a minute, then the line started to move. "See ya," DeSean called over his shoulder. She sulked and sauntered off.

As we followed the snaking line, DeSean tried impressing me by identifying the basketball shoes that other kids were wearing. "Look at those," he'd say, pointing nonchalantly. "Those are KD 11s."

It was a good way to keep his mind off the test—stress prevention—so I played along. "Are you sure? I don't know. They look more like 10s."

Pretty soon we were at the clerk's window, where we presented his documents, signed some paperwork, and were directed to the testing center. Randy had rejoined us.

"Good luck, buddy." I gave him a thumbs up, and he shot us a half-grin before heading back on his own.

***

I remember the first day DeSean came to Shelby Traditional with his foster mom, an older lady dressed in a lime green polyester pants suit. She was heavyset, and her full crown of white hair had a bluish hue. In fact, she looked more like a grandmother than a mother to him. She was enrolling him in first grade and getting bus information. The school year had started a few weeks earlier, but it wasn't unusual in our district for students in foster care to enroll later. Children in the system were often removed from the home unexpectedly due to neglect or drug use.

During the few minutes that I lingered in the front office, DeSean chatted with his foster mom while peering out at her from behind dark-framed glasses that complimented his bookish manners. He seemed highly attentive, perhaps on guard as a result of his former home life. I wasn't sure. But I would get to know him better in the weeks ahead.

As part of my counseling duties, I led sessions in the classroom that focused on behavior and social skills. The day I visited DeSean's first-grade class, I was talking to students about honesty, explaining, for example, the difference between telling the teacher something she needed to know and tattling on another student. I quickly noticed how introspective DeSean seemed, based on his line of questioning. He was quite inquisitive and wanted to know the finest of details. His level of comprehension seemed much higher than a first grader's. He expressed some reservations about "telling" on other students. I understood from his careful verbiage that he had grown up in neighborhoods that valued loyalty over "snitching," no matter what the neighbor's offense might have been.

Throughout the school day whenever I saw DeSean in the lunchroom or hallways, he was quiet and reserved and followed all the rules. But every day after school for those first few weeks, when I was on bus duty, he would waltz over, give me a high five, and impulsively, excitedly break into a run. I had to call after him, "DeSean, slow down!"

I learned more about DeSean during his annual review when I met with his foster mom and his first-grade teacher, which is when I learned why he was receiving speech therapy services. He had been a selective mute. I also learned that he had missed sixty days of kindergarten, which is one of the reasons he had been removed from the home.

I remember with clarity the cool November day when DeSean asked me to adopt him. I was making my rounds in the cafeteria during lunch, chatting with students, asking how their day was going. I stopped at DeSean's table to have a conversation with a pair of boys regarding their morning behavior. DeSean was a few seats away and waved me over.

"When are you coming back to our class to talk again?" He looked up at me, dark eyes shining with longing.

"In a couple weeks," I said.

He nodded and licked his lips. "That little girl who was with you at the Fall Festival, was that your daughter?"

I smiled at his reference to Kenzie. "Yeah, it was."

"Do you have any other kids?"

"Yes, I have twin boys."

"The ones in the picture in your office?"

"Yep. That's them."

"Did you adopt them?"

I nodded. "Yes, I did."

Just then another student approached and asked me to open her ketchup, and our conversation ended.

At the end of the day, I saw DeSean heading for his bus. "Have a good evening," I called after him. He smiled and waved at me.

I had moved on to watch students boarding another bus when I felt a tug on my coat. I turned to find DeSean standing there.

"Hey, you don't want to miss your bus." I pointed and gave him a little pat on the head.

But DeSean just stood there gazing up at me. "You want to adopt me?"

I tried not to respond with a facial expression or body language that might hurt his feelings, but I was stunned and unsure of what to say. I took his question seriously, as I knew he was sincere in asking. The truth was, Randy and I had had conversations about adopting another child—an older child, because we didn't feel up to raising another baby. I would have to discuss the matter with him.

Meanwhile, DeSean seemed rooted to the spot on the sidewalk, waiting for my response. I was worried at this point that he really would miss his bus.

I smiled at him. "That would be awesome! Now get on your bus, little buddy!"

His big, beautiful grin made my heart feel as though it would bust wide open. I rubbed his curly head and ushered him off. He walked to the foot of the bus and waved back at me before boarding.

He had noticed everything—Mackenzie, the twins' picture, my logical approach to behavior issues. I was flattered, but even more than that, I was amazed at DeSean's attentiveness and how he had sensed that our home revolved around one central rule: love one another.

I moved on quickly and turned into the wind, hoping to dry my eyes before anyone noticed the tears that had spilled down my cheeks.

***

When DeSean returned from the testing center twenty minutes later, he was moping as though he had failed.

Randy looked at me, then squinted at DeSean. "What the—"

DeSean broke into a grin. "I passed!"

We high-fived him and paraded back to processing to get his permit made. A few minutes later, we left together. In the parking lot of the DMV, Randy turned to DeSean.

"Wanna drive home?" he asked.

"Right now?" There was the slightest hesitation in his tone.

Randy chuckled. "Yeah, right now."

DeSean looked out across the parking lot to the highway beyond, the flow of traffic heavier than it had been when we arrived several hours earlier. He shrugged. "Sure. Why not?"

It was rush hour. Cars were bouncing like pinballs across all six lanes of the Watterson Expressway from Taylorsville Road to the next exit on the route, Interstate 64. DeSean maneuvered the BMW from one busy freeway to another, vigilant of his speed, the vehicles around him, and the ramp ahead.

"He did great," Randy told me later at the house. "Took it slow and easy. No problems at all."

I wagged my head in wonder, feeling happy that our son had completed this crucial rite of passage, yet feeling melancholy over him taking one more step toward adulthood and independence from us.

What had happened to that inquisitive little man I once knew, the first grader with all the questions, the child with an unquenchable thirst for life?

I closed my eyes and remembered the dark boy with the shy smile and a wish for the love of a family. I knew he was ready for the world, and I tried to make my peace with that. I prayed hard. I prayed the world would be good to him.

23: Live from the Fishbowl

Paul

I will never forget the day we found out our case would be heard by the Supreme Court. Our attorneys had filed the appeal in November, not long after the Sixth Circuit overturned Heyburn's ruling. Although we were hopeful, and there were murmurings among scholars and legal experts about cases similar to ours working their way through the appeals process, we were stunned by the news when it finally came on a Friday morning in mid-January.

I was at school that day. We had just come off winter break. I was in my office reading email and planning my day when Randy called.

"You're not going to believe this," he said. His voice was low and tense, so I couldn't tell if the news was good or bad.

"What? What is it?"

"We're going to the Supreme Court."

My heart thudded in my chest. I held my hand against it. "You're lying."

"I'm not lying. It's true. I just got a call from Shannon. It's probably on the Internet by now."

While we tossed words of disbelief back and forth to each other, I checked a news site and found out that the SCOTUS had accepted cases from Kentucky, Ohio, Michigan, and Tennessee, which would be combined and renamed *Obergefell v. Hodges*. The SCOTUS would consider two questions related to the Fourteenth Amendment: *1) Does the Fourteenth Amendment require a state to license a marriage between two people of the same sex? 2) Does the Fourteenth Amendment require a state to recognize a marriage between two people of the same sex when their marriage was lawfully licensed and performed out-of-state?* Our case was apparently the only one that raised both questions since we had plaintiffs not only attempting to marry in Kentucky, but plaintiffs who wanted their marriages that were performed outside of Kentucky recognized.

The rest of the day passed in a blur. I was preoccupied by thoughts of our next steps and, once again, how the media exposure would affect our private lives. I was nervous as well as excited. The Johnson-

Campion fishbowl was about to get tipped, sloshed, and ogled like never before. It seemed the harder we worked to live like a normal American family, the more we needed to be in the public spotlight. To be treated equally, ironically, required great scrutiny.

The weeks that followed were jam packed with meetings with our attorneys and interviews with dozens of news outlets. A few days after the announcement, the ACLU offered to join our case and James Esseks, the head of the LGBT Project, flew in from New York City to meet with the Kentucky plaintiffs and attorneys on behalf of the organization.

"We are happy to join you in this effort," Esseks told us over drinks in a private room at the Corner Café, a cozy little restaurant in Louisville's pampered East End. "Based on the history of gay rights and the same-sex marriage movement, who could ever have predicted Kentucky would play such a significant role in the matter?"

We soon got word that the Supreme Court would hear oral arguments in April, and a decision would likely be made by the end of June. Everything seemed to be happening at such a dizzying rate that we felt as if we were on a wild amusement park ride. In preparation for the onslaught of media interest, the legal team gave us talking points and coached us on such subtleties as word choice—for example, using the term "marriage" instead of "gay marriage." They also cautioned us about negative publicity and taught us the best ways to respond to the opposition.

The phone calls, emails, and text messages started rolling in. Among the higher profile stories we did were interviews with National Public Radio, *The Guardian*, the Danish Broadcasting Corporation, and Univision, the American Spanish language broadcast network. With the ACLU's help, Tevin launched a blog to document our journey to the Supreme Court called "My Two Dads," which drew the attention of MTV, Buzzfeed, and *The Huffington Post*. I was glad to see this new focus and hoped the public would find our son's perspective enlightening. In early April, Randy and Tevin flew out to California to take part in a special panel for law students at Stanford University. One of the law professors there had his clinic students focus on the SCOTUS case and had instructed them to prepare briefs to support our cause, then the university invited the plaintiffs and attorneys to visit so that the students could see the impact their work would have on real people. Since I couldn't miss school, Tevin traveled with Randy and was able to offer the students and others gathered to hear the panel the perspective of being raised by gay dads. Tevin had a compelling story to share, and I was proud to hear that he was so well received at Stanford. In fact, Randy told me that a couple of the professors asked if Tevin planned to go to law school.

"I wish I could have been there," I said with a sigh.

***

In late March, a crew from PBS came out to spend the day with our family. They were producing a short day-in-the-life film on two Kentucky families from opposite sides of the spectrum on the same-sex marriage issue. Martin Cothran's family would represent the conservative Christian view. Cothran worked for the Family Foundation of Kentucky and had been instrumental in getting the Defense of Marriage Act on the voting ballot in Kentucky in 2004. The show's producers explained that our families would be profiled side by side without any running commentary. In a separate shoot, Randy and I had been asked a series of questions on our backgrounds, how we met, our family values, and how the marriage ruling could affect us. That footage would be woven into the day-in-the-life profile. The producers assured us that both sides would get equal treatment, giving viewers an objective look at the issue.

"You know, this will be a good opportunity to show people that we're just like any other family," Randy pointed out as he fluffed his pillow in bed the night before. "People will finally get to see for themselves that the family with two gay dads is just as regular and boring as any other family."

I chuckled. "That's true."

The next morning, the crew arrived—two producers and a videographer. They immediately set to work getting us "miked up" so that we could go about our morning routines. They filmed us making breakfast and talking to the kids. Tyler was planning a trip to New York City for spring break, and Mackenzie and DeSean were gearing up for a vacation at Daytona Beach with Randy and me.

After breakfast DeSean and I put on our jackets and went outside to shoot hoops. The crew also got some footage of us walking the dogs, and later they rode with us to a hibachi grill for dinner.

Although they were pleasant to work with, I was glad when the film crew departed that evening. "That was exhausting."

"Tell me about it." Randy plopped down next to me on the couch. "Let's send the kids to bed early," he suggested.

Kenzie sounded off from the other room. "But it's Saturday!"

"Never mind," I said. "I'm the one going to bed early."

Randy threw an arm around me. "I think we did great, Dad." He kissed my cheek.

"I agree," I said, patting his leg. "The kids, too. I'm so proud of them."

***

Although we continued answering questions for the press and granting interview requests, our next major media event wasn't until June at the Robert H. Jackson Center, a museum and hall in my hometown of Jamestown, New York, dedicated to advancing public awareness of justice and the law. Randy and I had been asked to appear as featured guests in a discussion on marriage equality.

The folks at the center had asked me for the names of a hundred people to invite to the event, and I had obliged, including among them my father, brothers, and sisters, although I tried not to get my hopes up. And sure enough, after getting an invitation, one of my devout Catholic brothers explained to me via text message why he could not attend the event, how that would be going against the teachings of the church.

I was tired of the "one man, one woman" argument, which made no sense to me. How did same-sex relationships hurt anyone? Was the inability to procreate really an issue for the twenty-first century, with so many unwanted, adoptable children being born all over the world? Why not use our God-given free will to discuss the matter logically?

But there was no talking my brother down from his religious pedestal. The ACLU's media training on handling the opposition turned out to be of greater use to me in dealing with my own family than in dealing with the general public.

I decided to call my father the week before the event. I suspected that this had been a topic of conversation among him and most of my siblings. But I didn't care. I wanted to hear it from him. I wanted him to at least attempt to explain his position.

"Oh, yes, the Jackson Center," he said over the phone, and I could hear him exhale. "We need to talk about that."

"What is there to talk about?" I asked.

"Well, as the patriarch of the family, and because of my religious convictions, I cannot publicly support you in this." His speech was slow and deliberate.

I said nothing for a moment. Although I wasn't surprised, I was still disappointed. There is nothing quite like the feeling of a parent's rejection. Part of me wanted to hide, to retrieve the secret cloak of my youth and retreat to the bathroom to wallow in my sorrow. Another part of me wanted to shout in my father's face. How could he do this to me?

"I'm sorry to hear it. I've got to go."

"Goodbye, Paul."

When I hung up, I felt the prickly sensation of a slap where the phone had been.

*

By the time we traveled to Jamestown in June, we had been through a whirlwind of activity, most notably the unforgettable experience of hearing the oral arguments at the Supreme Court in Washington, D.C. The media coverage had been overwhelmingly favorable, and I was grateful to have had Randy at my side through it all.

Mackenzie and DeSean traveled with us to the Jamestown event, which was recorded live and posted on the Jackson Center's website. Professor John Barrett gave an overview of *Bourke v. Beshear* and the other cases, as well as their relevancy to the Jackson Center. Afterward Greg Peterson from the Jackson Center conducted the interview with Randy and me.

I was initially nervous in front of the crowd of several hundred attendees, but Greg was a calming force in the vast auditorium, and soon my attention was focused solely on him and the casual talk we were having—about growing up in Jamestown, my high school sports career, meeting Randy and understanding my calling in life. It was an odd experience—a conversation that was about me, but wasn't only about me; it was a conversation for the ages. The tale of Everyman, Everywoman. As I sat in the friendly glow of lights with my soul mate at my side, and my eyes drifting back again and again to the place where Mackenzie and DeSean were seated in the audience, I could not stop smiling inside. Everything seemed right.

Then suddenly, while Randy was describing our "family constellation," as he liked to call it, an image came to mind of another family—a different family, an isolated star in a universe all its own. A family of stubborn faith and firmly sealed lips. The family I had grown up with—the siblings I never really knew, the mother we lined up to kiss goodnight who blessed us before bed, the emotionally distant father focused on winning the bread for our family. I looked around for evidence of that iconic American family, and with a mixture of melancholy and relief found none. A couple of my siblings were there—Katie and Jim—but Mike, who couldn't make it that evening, and Katie were the ones who had chosen love over fear, who walked in the shadows and pondered every shade of gray. My father was missing. So were one of my sisters and four of my brothers. As proud as I was of my own family, the family I had made with the love of my life, I ached for the comfort of my flesh and blood at that moment, the blessing of my mother and father.

Despite my disappointment, that evening at the Jackson Center was one of the happiest moments of my life. When the program ended, we mingled with the audience, many of whom were family friends and old acquaintances from my younger years in Jamestown. A few were significant role models from my past, including my high school coach, Vere Lindquist, and my English teacher, Ms. Whitehead, who had written that encouraging note so many years before: *"You have an amazing life ahead of you.... You are the author of your life."*

There were people I didn't know, people I'd never met who had come from hundreds of miles away to hear us speak—strangers who lifted me up with their love and support. Meeting them and hearing some of their stories was humbling and gratifying in a way I never expected.

There were transgender people who waited in line to shake our hands and let us know our involvement in the case was making a difference for them. "I just want to thank you for all you've done for the LGBTQ community," one of them said, extending a hand and offering the warmest smile anyone's ever given me.

An openly gay city councilmember was there, too, as well as a gay school superintendent and his partner. They were local. This was not the Jamestown I had known. The city had evolved and changed for the better, even though some of my family had not, nor had the church. Yet the sense of fellowship that night reminded me of my youth at Sts. Peter and Paul, where I was an altar boy. The nods and the handshakes, the ladies smelling of rosewater, the men cleanly shaven. The pretty girls I stared straight past, the young men who caught my eye.

I remembered how I would always arrive early at Sts. Peter and Paul, slipping into my black cassock, pulling over the white surplice, waiting in the vestibule for the deacon's signal. The organ's rich bellow and the echo of voices in the congregation would slow me on the procession to the altar. I would stop at my appointed spot, turn slowly, and with great effort, genuflect, my legs feeling like rubber. I remembered sitting and standing, standing and singing, the words floating up into one booming "Allelujah!", the bell ringing for communion, Father Pavlock's muttered prayer over the host and the chalice.

I remembered being still, while my eyes roamed, searching, searching, searching the sanctuary for my father. The other father. The one who never really knew me. Who wasn't here now, at this moment, one of the happiest moments of my life.

And I did then what I had always done. I quieted my heart, and I stopped looking.

24: Accidental Activists

Paul

The trip to Washington, D.C., to hear our case argued before the Supreme Court started out like a family vacation. We set off early Sunday morning in my new king cab Ford F-150—Randy in front with me, and Tevin, Mackenzie, and DeSean in back; Tyler had been cast in *Music Man* with the Cincinnati Pops and had stayed behind for the production's dress rehearsal.

The Bluegrass was in full bloom, with lush green fields and bright pink redbuds all along Interstate 71. We made frequent stops for snacks, to stretch our legs, and to take in the intoxicating beauty of God's creation. We had perfect driving weather with clear, sunny skies the whole 600 miles, which seemed symbolic of our family's morally inspired journey, to foretell a clear path to victory, a happy ending for us and a new beginning for our country. By the time we crossed into Pennsylvania and hit the foothills of the Allegheny Mountains, we were so giddy with excitement that the five of us sang along to Bruno Mars' "Uptown Funk."

We had planned ahead for Kenzie and DeSean to be excused from school for three days, and their teachers had been highly supportive. In fact, DeSean's principal at Trinity, Dan Zoeller, remarked in an email, "What an awesome civics lesson this will be."

I had hoped and prayed hard for this kind of change all my adult life, but I had never dreamed we would play a role in such a momentous way. Although we were special to each other, Randy and I knew we were not the only gay couple in the world who had fallen desperately in love, who wanted nothing more than to live like other families, without the drawbacks that were rooted in discrimination over who we loved. I was thrilled to be part of the movement, but I was aware of the fact that Randy and I were mere cogs in the wheel of justice. I did not consider myself valiant. I did not think I was a hero, although I knew what it meant to face persecution. And I understood strength in numbers, the exponential power that Randy provided when he came into my life. Together we were a force for good in the world. That, I was certain of. But heroes? In the days and weeks ahead, our friends .

and family members and even some strangers would say so. But when I looked back on the impetus behind the conflicts we engaged in, the role I saw myself in time and time again was that of parent. So if I was a hero, I owed it to my children.

***

We had had a flurry of media requests for interviews and photos since January, when the Supreme Court announced it would hear our case. As much as I wanted to shy away from the cameras and microphones, the publicity had turned out to be a good thing for us; as Randy had predicted, the media coverage had proven an effective way to illustrate the fact that we were a regular American family. Interviews with *The Huffington Post* and PBS had already helped us make our case.

Fortunately for Randy and me, our son was assisting with the media campaign. Not only was Tevin recording our legal adventure on his blog, "Tevin's Two Dads," but he was offering skeptics of same-sex marriage the fresh perspective of an educated, intelligent, and promising young man who had been raised by gay men. And the world was tuning in as though it was a Super Bowl game.

By the time we arrived at the hotel in D.C., MSNBC had contacted Tevin about doing a live interview at the station the following morning. We were a little nervous about the arrangements.

"They're sending a camera crew," Tevin told us after checking a message on Twitter from Justin Oliver, who booked guests for "The Rundown with José Díaz-Balart."

"Nix that," he said. "They're sending a car for me."

Early the next day, Randy went with Tevin to meet the driver and make sure everything seemed legitimate. He came back to the room with a huge grin on his face. "They sent a chauffeur in an Escalade Limousine."

"Wow," I said. "Tevin had to love that!"

Kenzie grunted jealously with her hands on her hips.

DeSean gave a thumbs up. "Cool!"

"I checked his ID, too. It's all good. He said he'd bring him back to the hotel in an hour or two."

We gathered around the TV in our hotel room to watch Tevin's interview. When he appeared on the screen, we all shouted for joy and clapped as though we were watching U of L kick ass in a basketball game.

Tevin looked poised and professional in his fuchsia shirt and dark gray tie and jacket. Behind him was the slightly blurred image of the Capitol Building, the crowns of trees edging the bottom of the screen. All at once, it hit me. Here was our son on live TV in Washington, D.C. Goose bumps raced up my arms and down my back. I reached over and grasped Randy's hand. He smiled and shook his head, and I could see in his eyes how proud he was at that moment.

When Díaz-Balart asked what Tevin hoped to accomplish with his Tumblr blog, what he hoped to show the world, he calmly responded, "That we're just like everybody else. We're human. We're people. We're not freaks."

And what did Tevin have to say to those who believed that children should be raised by a mother and a father?

"I really have to challenge their mind set. My parents have given me a great life. And I could not have had that if they hadn't adopted me."

Randy and I looked at each other, both of us squeezing back tears. "That was unbelievable," I said.

"Oh my God, tell me about it." Randy's voice cracked with emotion.

When Tevin returned to the hotel, we threw our arms around him and practically hoisted him in the air the way teammates do in admiration of their star player. Tevin chattered about the experience and fretted over how he had appeared on the air.

"They want me to come back Wednesday morning for another interview."

"Are you going?" Randy asked.

We joked with him, nudging and punching his arm as though he'd been asked out on a date.

Tevin smiled and shrugged. "Yeah, I guess so."

Kenzie and DeSean whooped for joy, and Randy and I clapped him on the back.

We had planned to squeeze in some sightseeing when we got to D.C., but when we heard about marriage equality supporters camped out in front of the Supreme Court Building for tickets to hear the oral arguments, we decided to head over to the line and express our gratitude. We got directions at the front desk and set off on foot, dressed comfortably in casual clothes.

Along First Street near the Supreme Court, throngs of people gathered with rainbow flags and marriage equality signs in anticipation of Tuesday's historic event. I was heartened by the crowds and the sight of so many upbeat, friendly faces. However, feeling wary of protestors, I gathered the kids together and warned them things could get ugly.

"And if they do, I just want you all to know that there may be people shouting unkind words, but we know they have their rights to their opinions, even if they aren't the same as ours," I said.

The three of them nodded, understanding what might soon transpire.

We started walking again, taking in all the sights and sounds and the party atmosphere that stood in stark contrast with the scene Randy and I had encountered some twenty years earlier as a young gay couple. In 1993, we had been in Washington for our first gay pride march together. We had feared for our lives in those days, when literal "gay bashing" was an issue across the country. People had sneered and spit at us, had called us names. The threat of physical harm followed us everywhere, fists drawing back and arms swinging up all around us, and we held our breath and stayed on guard, constantly watching over our shoulder. The scornful looks we got haunted us for weeks afterward. It was painful to remember.

No sooner had this tormenting memory begun melting away when I spotted a cluster of protestors along First Street and felt those cold stares on me once again, their eyes shooting through me like nails. I paused long enough to round up the kids but not before they heard for themselves the collective cries of "All fags go to hell!" and saw the gigantic sign showing two men kissing that read, "This is a sin!" with some scripture quoted next to it.

When I saw the look of dismay on Mackenzie's face, felt her shoulders trembling as I guided her along the sidewalk, I was outraged. I could not let this moment pass without showing her the right way, without fighting back. I stopped amid the protestors and gestured furiously for Randy to join me. He hurried over, looking confused, and when he started to speak, I closed in on him, wrapping him in my arms and covering his mouth with mine. A burst of applause drowned out the protestors' jeers, and Randy and I walked away, hand in hand, refusing to be weighed down by hate and anger. We pumped our fists, shouting, "Love will win!" as we marched out of the attack zone and back into the safety of the street just outside the Supreme Court.

We found the line waiters staked out in an orderly fashion in folding canvas chairs in front of the building. They greeted us with handshakes and hugs and thanked us, in turn, when we introduced ourselves as plaintiffs in the case.

That evening, our family attended the "Freedom to Marry" reception honoring all the plaintiffs in same-sex marriage lawsuits across the country. Randy and I got to shake hands with Evan Wolfson, the father of the marriage equality movement, and the founder and president of Freedom to Marry. We'd met Evan briefly in Louisville during a town forum on marriage equality at the First Unitarian Church, a year earlier. He was reserved and polite at the reception when we introduced him to Tevin, DeSean, and Mackenzie.

"What a lovely family," he remarked.

"We're so pleased to meet you," Randy said. "We're just grateful for all you've done over the years for families like ours."

"Oh, it's been an honor, I assure you," he said, and he bowed ever so slightly before a crush of new arrivals waded in, forcing us aside.

That night, we also met two women we highly admired—journalist Nina Totenberg and civil rights attorney Gloria Allred. An aide to President Obama gave a speech noting that the President supported us and that he regretted being unable to attend due to a visit by the Japanese prime minister. It was a lovely and memorable evening, and we left feeling more optimistic than ever about winning the case.

Back at the hotel that night, we chased the kids to bed and immediately changed out of our suits. We had a long day ahead of us the next day and wanted to get a good night's sleep. Despite our good intentions, Randy and I ended up talking late into the night, recounting the day's events and wondering how everything would play out in the morning.

"It's just amazing to be where we are. Did you ever dream it would come to this?" Randy searched my face for an answer.

I shook my head. "No," I admitted. Everything had happened so quickly. Yet, I reminded myself, it had not happened quickly enough to save Matthew Shepard or to stop all the bullying against young gays and lesbians. I looked at Randy. It had not happened fast enough to spare us a lifetime of heartache. "But I did dream. We all dreamed. If we hadn't imagined a world like this, it never would have been possible."

Randy nodded and shut off the lights. It was difficult getting to sleep, with the energy of the city bristling all around me. Perhaps it would be harder to sleep from now on, with our dreams becoming reality.

***

On the day of the oral arguments, we met with our team of attorneys in a small conference room on the lower level of the Capitol Hill Suites. Some of the plaintiffs took the limited seats available while others gathered around the table, standing shoulder to shoulder in the cramped space. There were no windows, and the artificial lighting was dim. The low ceilings and high humidity made the room feel even smaller.

James Esseks stood at the head of the table looking cooler than the rest of us in a dark jacket and striped navy tie. "Thank you all for being here," he said, his clear, distinctive voice commanding our attention. "This is the day we've all been waiting for." His eyes scanned the room as he spoke, lingering thoughtfully over each one of us. "It wouldn't have been possible without your courage, your involvement, your willingness to stand up for equality in the face of adversity for so many years," he said. "All of you have felt the effects of unfair treatment, of being denied full marriage rights, of raising children without proper protections, of facing medical emergencies without being able to count on your spouse being recognized. It's time for the American values of freedom and equality to apply to all couples."

In a final rallying cry, James shook his fist and raised his voice. "Okay, let's do this!"

As the room erupted in whoops and applause, I quickly wiped the tears from the corners of my eyes and noticed some of the others doing the same.

Afterward the attorneys gave us an overview of what to expect as the day progressed and instructed us on the order in which we would march down to the Supreme Court Building, as well as what part of the oral arguments we would get to hear in the courtroom.

Joe Dunman, a young, bright-eyed attorney with an easygoing manner, explained how the process would work. "You'll get to hear the arguments for question number two," which was, *Does the Fourteenth Amendment require states to recognize legally valid same-sex marriages performed elsewhere?* Douglas Hallward-Driemeier would speak for the plaintiffs.

"When it's time, I'll lead our group down to the courtroom—the two of you, Greg and Mike, Luke and Jim, Kim and Tammy, and all the family members," he said, gesturing to the others.

We all nodded in agreement, and Joe moved along.

James Esseks left first, escorting Tim and Larry, and Maurice and Dominique to hear the first round of oral arguments on whether the Fourteenth Amendment required states to license a marriage between two people of the same sex. Mary Bonauto would present the plaintiffs' side.

Everyone was cheerful and chatty. The excitement in the room was palpable. We talked with the other plaintiffs and fussed over the kids. Randy helped Kenzie straighten her dress while I adjusted her hair band, tucking back a few loose curls. DeSean fiddled with his tie, and Tevin kept smoothing the lapels of his jacket. He had expressed some concerns earlier about snipers, while Kenzie confessed she was worried about encountering protestors.

Randy draped an arm around each of them. "We'll be fine, kids," he assured them, and he drew us all together for a group hug.

Soon Joe was corralling our team together and leading us out the door and into the muggy morning heat. We stayed close to the kids to ease their anxiety, but as we approached the Supreme Court Building, we were all overcome by the massive support shown by the crowds. Thousands of people with signs and banners filled three blocks along First Street. Much to Kenzie's relief, we noticed only a few protestors along the way, and they were lost in a sea of happy faces, barely visible in the shadows of bright, fluttering rainbow flags with their "Jesus Hates You" posters.

I checked my text messages. All morning, I had been communicating with my sister Katie and brother Mike, both of whom had traveled to D.C. with their spouses for the occasion. We were hoping to meet up before the oral arguments. I typed a quick message to Katie to let her know we were en route to the courthouse.

Along the way, Joe kept turning back to count heads, reminding me of a grade school teacher on a field trip. Occasionally he would stop to ensure we all stayed together.

The street in front of the Supreme Court Building was cordoned off, and security officers lined the steps leading up to the portico and its massive marble columns. The building was a formidable sight gleaming in the sunlight, and a sense of awe came over me as I gazed up at it and absorbed anew the significance of all the injustices that had been settled here. I spotted Katie and her husband Terry waving at us from the front of the crowd, and we rushed over to the curb.

After a quick round of hugs, I asked, "Have you seen Mike and Jim?"

We all turned and scanned the street and adjoining areas, now swarming with people. Katie and Terry shook their heads.

I wondered aloud where they could be. I checked my phone.

Katie frowned and rubbed my arm reassuringly. "They'll be here," she said.

A wave of gratitude flooded over me. Words could not convey my appreciation, but I tried anyway. "Thank you both so much for coming all this way."

Terry shrugged. "That's what family's all about."

"We wouldn't have missed it for the world," Katie insisted, her eyes glowing, her face flushed from the heat. "I'm so proud of you, Paul."

A knot formed in my throat. I tried to swallow it down, tried to speak, but could only shake my head and squeeze Katie's hand before Joe swooped between us and apologetically swept us away from the curb, guiding us to the side entrance of the building.

Tevin looked as dapper as ever in a dark suit with a fuchsia shirt and red-checkered tie, but his eyes shifted from the street crowds to the government grounds to the rooftops of the buildings around us. He adjusted his glasses and feigned a smile when he noticed me watching him. DeSean, who had also maintained his handsome state in a navy suit and white shirt, retreated into his phone. Although Kenzie was the most vocal among us concerning the oppressive heat, she was perhaps the least affected by it in terms of appearance. From where I stood, she looked as sweet and lovely as she had that morning at the hotel in a black dress and a short, white shawl vest. Now, however, she was growing restless, and she alternated between observing the rituals of the Supreme Court's police force and attempting to distract her edgy brother from the idea of sniper fire.

We stood outside the big bronze doors for several minutes until we were cleared to enter. The guard held the door for us, and we stepped inside the cool, spacious interior and descended a flight of stairs into the basement of the building where Joe told us to stay on the carpeted area. While waiting, we struck up a conversation with the other plaintiffs, chuckling about these strange instructions. Soon Tevin, Kenzie, DeSean, and the other family members in our group were escorted to the cafeteria while we were queued to enter the courtroom.

Not long after that, a commotion erupted on the main floor. The eight of us exchanged worried looks as shouts and the footfalls of someone running echoed above us. We heard officers scrambling and calling out orders, and then dead silence. Joe came down a moment later to assure us everything was fine.

"I hope Tevin's okay," I told Randy.

Joe looked up from his cell phone. "I promise, they're all fine," he said.

Later we learned that a protestor had disrupted the proceedings by yelling, "If you support same-sex marriage, you will burn in hell!" and had to be dragged out of the courtroom by security guards. Fortunately, that bit of news was withheld to keep from dampening our spirits. Before long we were on our way to the security checkpoint just outside the courtroom on the second floor. Randy and I were the last couple to go through the metal detector, where a security officer named Moses, after one of the greatest lawgivers in human history, cleared us to enter the giant, ornate double doors. The courtroom was brightly lit, adding even more grandeur to the white marble columns and red velvet drapes behind the mahogany bench. The black leather chairs of the nine justices were empty, but Randy and I had studied the seating chart and knew that we would be closest in proximity to Justice Kagan, the court's newest member. We were seated among several rows of pews near the front. Behind us were public viewing areas. Security officers covered the courtroom and were in constant motion, surveying every person in the room.

Within a few minutes, the justices entered the courtroom, and the great space filled with a restless sort of quiet; the only sounds were the rustle of robes and paperwork and the soft static of microphones coming to life. Randy winked at me, the corners of his mouth turning up slightly, and when he brushed against me, I realized how surreal the scene playing out before me seemed. A strange sensation surged through my body—a cold chill with a flash of insight. An image of Earth came to mind, a blue marble in deep black space, along with the feeling that I was shrinking into it, taking my rightful place in the world. I was struck with the notion that we were all tiny vessels in an ocean of possibility, that our planet was mostly water, fluid, always changing.

I tried my best to focus my attention on the history that was happening right before my eyes, to hear the logic and reasoning not only of Justice Ginsberg—when she spoke, all eyes turned to her, and a spirit of reverence took hold—but also to acknowledge the assertions of Justice Scalia on states' rights. In that hour, however, despite my intentions, my emotions roared silently within me as the whirlwind of events that had brought us here came back to me with sudden clarity— the hate and intolerance we had navigated all our lives to avoid; the grave storms that loomed over us, threatening the safety of our children; the cancer diagnosis that had seemed like the cold blue end of our happiness; the oncologist with the hard heart; the icy indifference of a health-care system that discriminated against us; the cold stares of school parents who questioned my "gay agenda;" the murky waters of the lawsuit we had joined against our state to have our California marriage recognized.

We had never intended to become activists. We had stumbled into that role simply trying to live our lives, to raise our children—to take them to the doctor, to help them get driver's licenses, to protect their future. Yet if I had learned anything in the last three years, it was that beneath the troubled waters of our lives lay an ocean of possibility. Within that ocean were the tiny ripples we had started.

I was thinking how every ripple mattered when Randy nudged me. He had noticed Justice Kagan looking directly at us. There was no mistaking her gaze meeting mine, no mistaking the smile that crossed her face, and I believed at that moment that change was imminent, that we had had a part in making it happen. I came back to my body then, back to my simple existence, back to the room where history was being made. I felt human again. I felt human perhaps for the first time.

***

When court adjourned, James rounded up Randy and me and the other couples to coach us on making a dramatic march down the front steps of the building. But before stepping out under the portico, we were reunited with our families. The kids were eager to hear how it went.

"Everything seemed to go very well," I told them. "James Esseks will be giving us a full report back at the hotel."

By this time, the Supreme Court's police force had put a damper on James' plans for marching down the steps with our arms raised in victory. Instead, we stood in a long row at the monumental entrance to the building and each couple took a turn stepping forward and raising their clasped hands in the air as throngs of supporters applauded below. When it was our turn, I felt slightly dizzy and exhilarated, as though I'd just finished a run. The scene beyond the plaza overwhelmed my senses: all along First Street and the sidewalk in front of the building were the happy faces of so many strangers looking up at us, colorful banners, signs bobbing up and down, and huge pride flags unfurling in the air. As I held onto Randy's hand, every hope I'd ever had for love and family—hopes I'd worn like a full suit of armor—fell away from me, and I was cloaked in the truth of everything I had now. I wished at that moment that the brilliance of this day would never end.

Amid the deafening roar of the crowd, we made our way down the steps to the plaza. After the attorneys for our case and some of the plaintiffs spoke to the media, we met up with Katie, Terry, Mike, and Jim. There were hugs all around, and together we walked back to the hotel in the stifling heat to rehydrate and refresh ourselves. Once there, back in the hotel conference room, James Esseks recapped the oral arguments and predicted that we were "nearing the end game" on the freedom to marry. "Everything looks good from our standpoint," he said, and he credited Mary Bonauto and Douglas Hallward-Driemeier for making the case before the justices. "We anticipate they will rule in our favor, and that decision should be handed down by late June."

A vigorous round of applause followed James' brief talk, and then we all dispersed to make our way to the luncheon the ACLU was hosting for plaintiffs and their families. My siblings and their spouses joined us and the kids, and we rode the Metro across town to the ACLU's office. It was a pleasant gathering, and we spent a relaxing afternoon eating and talking with family members, the other plaintiffs, and our attorneys.

I hated for the day to end and had to brace myself for painful goodbyes from Mike and Katie. They had been my closest siblings— my allies—over the years after my exile from the family, and I was sad to see them go, especially Katie.

"I can't thank you and Terry enough for coming all this way," I said.

"You don't have to," Katie said, her voice choking with emotion. She reached up to hug my neck.

As we stood there embracing, I remembered the anguish I felt saying goodbye to her in 1992, when I moved from Jamestown to Kentucky to be with Randy. At the time she was the only family I had left in Jamestown, the only one—it seemed to me then—who mourned my leaving our childhood home. I could feel my eyes filling with tears. I didn't want to let go for fear of the dam breaking, didn't want to look into her eyes and feel that way again—to feel gratitude as unbearable as the hurt, the long separation, months that rolled into years.

"Promise we'll get together again soon," I managed.

Katie smiled and nodded. "I love you, Paul." She kissed my cheek.

"I love you, too, Katie," I whispered, the words breaking in my throat, and suddenly I was a young man again, starting over, ready to run from that moment and never look back. We were weeping for all that was lost, for the pride that ripped our family apart, for all the love that could have been. My head swam with images of candles and altars, murmured prayers, my mother's bedtime blessings, her fingers pressing my heart.

When Katie turned to go, I knew by the look on her face that these goodbyes had been as painful for her as they had been for me. I couldn't speak. I lifted a heavy hand and waved goodbye.

***

We left D.C. the next day, after Tevin's live interviews at MSNBC and *The Huffington Post*. When the traffic thinned, somewhere in Virginia, we stopped and Randy took over driving. I checked my news feed and found out that Judge Heyburn had died. I told Randy. We were both quiet, but later I realized we were thinking the same thing. It was as though Heyburn had waited to hear the oral arguments at the Supreme Court supporting his decision before drifting away, his work in this world finished.

25: Love Wins

Randy

The week before the Supreme Court's ruling was expected, Paul and I took a much-needed vacation in New Orleans. Our lives had been moving at breakneck pace all year. We were drained from media interviews, special engagements, and consultations with our attorneys—on top of family and work obligations. When the first and only opportunity came for us to get away, we booked a hotel in the French Quarter and made the ten-hour drive from Louisville to Louisiana. We slept late every morning and splurged on beignets from Café du Monde, spent our days wandering along Bourbon Street with its sweaty, bead-draped bodies and street performers, then capped off the evenings by feasting on Cajun cuisine and patronizing bars with live jazz music.

It was a relaxing week, and the morning we checked out, we were both full up from jambalaya and craft beer and ready to head home. Our attorneys expected the Supreme Court decision to be announced Monday, and we had every reason to believe the ruling would be in our favor. So we'd planned to drive home Thursday, then have Friday and Saturday to recuperate before flying to D.C. on Sunday. The valet had brought the car around to the hotel lobby entrance.

The heat hit me as we exited through the revolving doors. "It's already muggy," I remarked, sliding behind the wheel.

Paul blew out a puff of breath, pulling the passenger door shut and buckling his seatbelt. "Whew! No kidding."

I quickly adjusted the mirrors, anxious to get on the road, but when I pressed the ignition button, nothing happened. "What the hell?" I glanced at Paul, who raised his eyebrows and waited silently. I knew something wasn't right. I tried again, and when the engine wouldn't turn over, I scanned the dashboard for warning indicators. Since nothing had happened when I pressed the ignition button, I suspected the battery, or worse, the starter, since other electrical features on the car seemed to function appropriately. The valet claimed that he didn't have any trouble starting the car. I called AAA Roadside Assistance, and the mechanic who came to the hotel confirmed that there was no issue with the battery. The car would have to be towed in for repair.

In the end, our travels home were waylaid by a failed starter. Paul and I rode in the tow truck from the hotel to the nearest BMW dealer and waited several hours for the starter to be replaced, a fix that required removing the BMW's motor. From the service center's waiting area, I called my niece Nicki, who was looking after Mackenzie, to let her know about our delay and sent text messages to DeSean and Tevin. Paul and I walked to a nearby restaurant called Bud's Broiler for lunch. The rustic A-framed building appeared to have been the place to get ice cream back in the day. Although the décor was somewhat dated, the restaurant prominently displayed pride in serving charcoal broiled burgers, and the food and service proved satisfactory. Back at the service center, Paul and I kept looking at the clock and recalculating the time we'd get home.

By three PM the car was fixed and the bill was squared away. I drove cautiously at first, in the event some mechanic forgot to tighten a bolt. But once I got onto the interstate, my confidence was restored. Nevertheless, it was painful to have spent thousands of dollars on a repair that had seemingly no effect on the car's performance. We updated the family on our estimated arrival time: one AM. It had been cloudy and humid all day, and as we drove out of Louisiana, I prayed we would have a clear shot home.

Somewhere along Interstate 65 North in the early evening, I got a phone call from Crystal Cooper of the ACLU. "Is there any way you and Paul could get on a flight to Washington tonight? We think there may be a decision announced tomorrow morning."

It felt as though my heart dropped into my stomach. "Tomorrow! Oh my God, seriously?" I looked at Paul. He was grinning, and I knew he must have heard what Crystal said. "We're on the road now driving back from New Orleans." Outside the driver's side window, I caught a glimpse of tall pine trees towering over the rural stretch of interstate highway.

"We won't get to Louisville until probably one or two in the morning." I told her. "There's really no way we can do it." I was exhilarated and dismayed at the same time.

There was a pause before Crystal's voice came back to me. "Do you think Tevin might be willing to represent you?"

"Tevin?" I glanced at Paul, who was looking back at me, nodding. "That's fine by us, if he wants to do it." The thought of Tevin taking on the role made me emotional. His involvement moved me like nothing else, and I'd found myself wondering again and again over the past few months, how did we get so lucky to have such a son, and when did he become such a warrior? I clenched my mouth to keep my jaw from trembling.

Crystal said she would contact him directly. She asked if Paul and I could plan to attend a press conference in Louisville, and I told her we wouldn't miss it.

After hanging up, I reached over and squeezed Paul's hand. I filled him in on the press conference. "This could be it, Dad. Tomorrow morning. Can you believe it?"

His voice wavered, and his gaze wandered to the view outside the passenger window. "I just hope it's the decision we're hoping for."

My first impulse was to berate him for being cynical, but I couldn't help feeling dubious myself. We had talked about the what-if's. We knew that we would go on with our lives, that we would keep fighting for the sake of our family and doing whatever it took to protect our children and ourselves from any wrong. Paul's concern was always about the struggle getting worse. I knew that was a very real possibility, but I didn't want to think about it.

Not long after my conversation with Crystal, Tevin called to get our advice on flying to Washington for the decision.

"Of course we want you to go," I assured him. "What a thrilling opportunity!"

"I definitely want to go, but the flight situation is crazy with all these storms we're having." He was talking fast, which I took as a sign of nervousness. "I'll probably get delayed on a connecting flight. Seems there's no way to avoid it. At least that's what they're telling me. But I'll be in a better position to get to D.C. from wherever I end up. If I don't take a flight out of Louisville tonight, I won't make it in time for the announcement."

Although I was worried, I tried to stay positive. "Sounds like an adventure."

Tevin laughed, a high, hearty laugh—a rowdy boy's kind of laughter—and I was reminded in that moment of his vulnerabilities, of all the ridicule and adversity he'd faced on our behalf. I recalled our trip to Washington together for the oral arguments, and everything he had done for us, and how brightly he'd shined in the spotlight. The best thing I might have ever done was playing some part in building the strength of his character. How else could I have earned this—to have been worthy of such profound love?

***

I thought back on the trip to D.C. The morning after the oral arguments, a limo had whisked Tevin off to MSNBC's studio for the first of two live interviews. From there, he'd gone to *The Huffington Post*'s bureau office for another live appearance.

After packing our bags, Paul and I had watched both segments from the hotel room, feeling particularly pleased with Tevin's delivery and how well he'd handled himself on camera. Afterward we'd loaded the truck and drove by the studio to pick him up.

Although it was only a short distance from the hotel to the studio, we probably could have walked there faster. It was lunch hour, and the crosswalks were flooded with pedestrians. By the time we reached Tevin, he was annoyed and uncomfortable from waiting in the heat.

"It's about time," he grumbled as he climbed in and slumped into his seat. His face was beaded with sweat.

Although the guilt of his long wait weighed on me, I tried to focus on the positive. "How did it feel, being in front of millions of people all over the country?"

Tevin shrugged and sat up a little. "Pretty good, actually."

"We've been wondering where you got the skill to keep that level of composure on live TV," Paul added.

Tevin rolled his eyes dramatically for Kenzie and DeSean's benefit, but I could see the corners of his mouth turning upward slightly.

I turned around in the passenger seat and gave Tevin a somber look. "We are seriously so proud of you, son."

"Yes, we are," Paul chimed in. "It means a lot to us that you're so willing to step up and speak out on the issue. You're putting yourself out there, and we know how scary that can be."

Tevin waved a hand dismissively. "I like doing it. It's good practice for me."

I gazed back at him, admiring his thoughtful eyes and firm jaw. Where had the chubby cheeks and sweet pucker gone? I wondered. Where had the time gone? "Watching you the last few days has been unreal," I told him. "I'm just amazed by your skill and your confidence. Aren't you, Dad?" I could feel the tears welling up, all the raw emotions of the week suddenly surfacing.

Paul nodded quickly, adjusting the rearview mirror. "Tevin, you were incredibly brave," he said, and he tilted the mirror, presumably to get a glimpse of Kenzie and DeSean, the smaller and equally good apples that we could, by some miracle, call our children. "All you guys were great." He reached across the seat and grabbed my hand. "We are so blessed," he said.

"Yes, we are." I stroked Paul's arm and gripped his palm tighter. The tears were flowing, heavy and warm on my cheeks. I let them spill out, imagined them filling a wishing well that reflected the faces of our family on its shining, rippling surface.

I wiped my eyes and turned around with a thought in mind— something to say to better express my love and appreciation. But the words stalled in my throat. Tevin's face was streaked with tears.

***

Later on the road, we heard from Tevin that he'd been laid over in Chicago for the night. At some point I got a text message that the press conference would be held at Dan Cannon's law office at eleven-thirty AM. It felt as if we would never get home. In Elizabethtown, forty-five miles south of Louisville, we were slowed by a thunderstorm. We could see the flash and glow of lightning for miles before the torrential downpour hit.

It rained the rest of the way, including when we stopped in Shepherdsville to pick up Mackenzie. Nicki and her husband Dustin had waited up for us, but the kids were sleeping, and I had to rouse

Kenzie from a makeshift pallet of blankets that someone had made with the news of our setback. As I led our drowsy daughter to the car, Dustin followed us out with a big umbrella. We pulled into our garage at two-thirty AM, gathered what we could in a single load, and headed straight for bed.

The next morning, we got up and started milling around making coffee and cleaning up. I unpacked half my bag, mainly to find my toothbrush and electric razor. After washing up and getting dressed, Paul turned on CNN in the bedroom. I lay across the bed checking my phone, clicking the refresh button on the SCOTUS blog every thirty seconds.

At a minute past ten, there was a brief pause when I hit refresh, and my phone's screen flickered before the headline appeared: "Love Wins!"

I screamed "Yes!" and jumped out of bed. "We won!"

"Are you sure?"

"It's right here, on the SCOTUS blog!" I held up my phone.

Paul pulled up the site on his own phone and skimmed the content, his face flushed, eyes wider and brighter than I'd ever seen them. "I want confirmation."

"We won, Dad!" I leaned over to hug his neck and kiss his cheek. "Why's that so hard to believe?"

Suddenly Wolf Blitzer was on CNN making the announcement and rolling live footage of the scene outside the Supreme Court, where jubilant crowds erupted in cheers, waving rainbow flags and "Love Wins!" signs in the air. The Gay Men's Chorus of Washington broke into "The Star-Spangled Banner," and people were embracing—gay couples and straight couples, lesbians and allies—it was hard to distinguish who was who, and, praise God, it no longer mattered. Love was love. I was crying myself, and I noticed Paul brushing away tears as we watched the coverage, scanning the masses for any sign of Tevin.

At that moment, we got a text from our son, confirming everything we were seeing on television. Soon our cell phones and house phone were exploding. Paul took a call from Jamestown radio personality Jim Roselle and did a live interview on the air, which he had promised to do earlier that month while in Jamestown. After he finished up the interview, we basked in the celebration on CNN. We listened to Jim

Obergefell, who was standing in front of a bank of microphones on the steps of the Supreme Court. Just behind him stood our Tevin, tall and proud, smiling from ear to ear. It was an amazing experience to see our son on national television celebrating marriage equality. We held each other and cried and trembled with joy.

As I was scrambling to get Mackenzie ready to go to the press conference, I answered a call from my brother Willie.

"I just want you to know how proud I am of you for standing up for what you believe in." Willie's voice was deep and somber. I thought I detected a note of melancholy in it, as though he regretted not having told me this sooner. "Congratulations."

I stopped in the hallway and stared at the photos of our children, their faces aglow, and of Paul and me, always in the center. I had never doubted that we were a family, worthy of the same treatment as other families. Willie's words gave me hope that the rest of the world might be able to see us now for who we were.

All the hurt I had ever known—as a boy, as a brother, even as a father—balled up in my throat, and I choked on the knot it formed while trying to speak. I took a deep breath. My voice shook. "Thank you, Willie," was all I could manage.

26: A New Tradition

Randy

The days and nights following the marriage equality ruling melded into one long celebration filled with hugs and handshakes, champagne toasts, and messages of appreciation that poured in from around the world to Paul and me and the other plaintiffs, thanking us for standing up for the rights of gay and lesbian couples. We were moved by the overwhelming show of support, and we rode that wave of emotion like an unstoppable current to higher ground where our faith in the power of love grew even stronger. For two decades, Paul and I had been climbing toward this symbolic summit to be recognized as parents, our mutual ambition. And now we had reached it. Now we were on that mountaintop. We were officially a family.

It seemed impossible, yet unquestionable—the only just outcome. Every morning I woke up thinking I must still be dreaming, to be able finally to call the man in bed next to me my husband, to complete our lives as formal soul mates, and to know that the children we'd loved and nurtured and raised together were acknowledged now as ours, together. Everything was as it should be, as I had always stubbornly believed that it should be, but even so, I was grateful to awaken every day to this new reality.

Paul and I were still high on higher love the following weekend, when we drove out to the family farm in West Point, Kentucky, for a Fourth of July celebration. My nephew Mackie, Myrtle's son, had bought the old homestead and acreage from my five siblings and me to keep the farm in the family. Mackie had fixed up the faded blue-gray tobacco barn, bush-hogged the land, and invited us out for a picnic and fireworks.

We arrived with Mackenzie and DeSean on that sweltering Saturday to a welcoming setup of tailgating tents, coolers packed with ice and beverages, and a full spread of food arranged on tables inside the newly renovated barn.

Outside the barn, a few relatives and friends rushed to greet us. "Congratulations, you two," Phyllis chimed, hugging each of us. "I'm so happy for you."

"Thank you," I said. "It's still so surreal to us." The muscles in my mouth ached from smiling so much. I reached over and squeezed Paul's arm, resisting the urge to pull him closer. Sweat trickled down my temples.

Two more familiar faces sidled up next to us—Janie and Kathy, lifelong family friends.

"Hey, I saw you guys on the news. Great job!" Janie said.

Just then, a guy I was sure I'd seen before offered his hand, and I shook it, digging deep into my memory, sorting through names and faces that I'd thought best to forget after my troubled adolescence until a flicker of recognition flared to life. "You must be Steve, Matt Warner's brother," I said, knowing Steve was a friend of Mackie's. We were all pretty close in age and had gone to the same high school.

"No, actually I'm Matt."

"I'm sorry," I said quickly. "I haven't seen you in thirty years!"

Matt waved off my apology and tossed in another compliment about our involvement in the marriage equality case. Paul and I thanked him and moved on, exchanging greetings with some of the other guests. Much to my chagrin, conversations with family members were as awkward as ever. Although many of my kin were eager to express their admiration, some of those same people disagreed with our "lifestyle," as they called it. Their condemnation manifested in their sidelong glances and the uncomfortable silences that followed their words of congratulations. It was unsettling, but I was determined to keep the mood celebratory.

We helped ourselves to hamburgers and fresh fruit and sat at one of the tables with Myrtle, Violet, and my nephew Brian. My nieces, Tina, Nicki, Kelly, and Julie, sat at the adjoining table.

Aunt Vera, who was sitting nearby, joined our conversation. She was in her eighties and very energetic, always wearing a smile that could light up the room. She was dressed in blue jeans and a light blouse with colorful flowers. "Randy, there's something Aunt Teatta and I made for you and Paul up at the house."

I set my fork down and wiped my mouth, giving her my full attention. "What's that, Aunt Vera?"

Violet smiled and clasped her hand over her mouth in mock surprise. "It's a quilt!"

Aunt Vera nodded, her eyes locking on mine. "Yes, it's a wedding quilt. It's up in the house there, in a plastic bag on the table."

I felt my jaw drop, and I turned to Paul.

He patted my hand. "Go get it," he said.

My eyes started to water, and my throat closed up. I couldn't speak.

Violet and the others were chattering about their wedding quilts, recalling how fond they were of those gifts. It was a tradition in our family, had been a tradition for years. I'd mentioned that I wanted one after our engagement twenty-four years earlier. My resentment had been more pronounced after Paul and I married in Palm Springs in 2008. It was a point of pride and a show of affection. I'd been bitter about being excluded. I'd wondered, were Paul and I not worthy of that love—of sharing in such a tender, intimate custom?

Stunned and happy, I got up from the table and went to the house. I found the quilt on the table and slipped it gently from the protective plastic, clutching it as if it were a lost child, then smoothing it out against the table to admire the artistry. The quilt was crafted in red and white fabrics, with cardinals and other emblems symbolizing the passion that Paul and I had long shared for U of L sports. I recognized material from one of my mother's blouses and the ache of her absence flared up inside me—the years she had missed, the joy of grandchildren, the love of family. I tried to imagine what she might say to me now, how she would reconcile the bigotry in our bloodlines, whether I could keep finding room in my heart to forgive knowing that's what she would have wanted.

I tucked the quilt back in its plastic bag and carried it out the door. My brother Jim was heading inside as I came out. I held the door for him, and he caught it, thanking me. But before he could duck inside, I stopped and blocked him on the porch stoop, cradling the bundled quilt in my arms.

"I got my quilt, Jim." I looked him in the eye, and he looked back at me without a word or a nod or even the slightest smile. "It took twenty-four years and a trip to the Supreme Court, but I got it." I clenched the bagged quilt in my fists and held it up for him.

Jim said nothing. He blinked at me, stood silently with his mouth drawn tight, holding the door, waiting for me to move.

I stepped off the porch and walked away without looking back—moving forward instead, taking the lightest steps I've ever taken. I could see Paul just ahead at a picnic table in his Cardinals baseball cap.

I remembered when I first laid eyes on him under the dizzying swirl of disco lights, how I knew right away that his heart was good. How I knew there was some sort of magic in our meeting there, that it hadn't happened by accident. And now that sensation grabbed me again, the most pure and radiant love—an energy from some other world, a place I couldn't fathom. A place from which my mother watched and nodded her approval.

I opened the quilt on Paul's lap while my sisters called over DeSean and Mackenzie. "Your daddies got their wedding quilt. Come see!"

My brother Bobby and some others ambled over.

"Guess what I got?" I pointed to the quilt, which Paul was holding and admiring. "I got my quilt. I finally got it."

Bobby shrugged and took a drink from his red Solo cup. "That's okay. I got two."

I wanted to laugh out loud. I wanted to shake my head and point a finger at him. But it just didn't matter. I only needed one. One was all I would ever need.

Afterword

Higher Love is intended to impact three specific groups: 1) LGBTQ (Lesbian, Gay, Bisexual, Transgender, Questioning) youth coming to terms with their sexual orientation and struggling to reconcile this with their potential desires to create a family of their own; 2) Families of those struggling with accepting their loved one's sexual orientation; and 3) Children of LGBTQ parents.

Institutionalized and internalized homophobia can be extremely detrimental to one's psychological well-being. Many struggle with their sexual orientation as a result. During that tumultuous time in their lives, having a resource that shows how each can choose to live their lives openly and honestly can be instrumental in their future happiness. Acknowledging the struggles associated with building a family led by a same-sex couple, we hope Higher Love offers a perspective that this group will find valuable. They will see that it is certainly possible for a same-sex couple to commit their lives to each other and create a loving home for children, with integrity.

Research has shown that suicidal ideation and suicide attempts are more common in LGBTQ youth than the general population. According to the Center for Disease Control, via the Trevor Project, suicide is the second leading cause of death among young people ages ten to twenty-four, and LGB youth are four times more likely, and questioning youth are three times more likely, to attempt suicide as their heterosexual peers. Higher Love offers those struggling with their sexual orientation an example of how they, too, can be happy and LGBTQ at the same time.

Parents sometimes find difficulty in accepting their LGBTQ youth. In fact, the Trevor Project notes that as much as forty percent of the homeless youth in the United States identify as LGBTQ, secondary to family rejection. According to a study conducted at San Francisco State University, researchers have established a clear link between accepting family attitudes and behaviors toward their LGBT children and better overall health in adulthood. It shows that specific supportive behaviors can protect against depression, substance abuse, and suicidal behavior in early adulthood. Our hope is that *Higher Love* can offer an optimistic perspective for parents of LGBTQ youth that may foster an understanding that facilitates accepting family attitudes.

An estimated 270,313 children in the United States live in households headed by same-sex couples. It is likely that many of them may feel isolated, as if their family is the only one struggling to "fit in". We believe that *Higher Love* can offer the perspective that others are faced with similar challenges and that their family should be valued as any other.

Paul Campion and Randy Johnson

Acknowledgements

~ PAUL CAMPION AND RANDY JOHNSON ~

We would like to thank Bobbi Buchanan for taking the time to listen to our stories and put together words that describe our journey. It has truly been a pleasure working with her on this project. Her hard work and determination is a sight to behold. She has become family to us and we love her, tremendously.

Thank you to Becky Tiller, graphic artist, who created the jacket for this book. She is a great friend with amazing talent.

William Kolb, photographer, has been a friend of our twins for a number of years. We appreciate his photos, which are featured on the cover. William is a kind young man with a very promising future.

We also would like to thank Deborah Baldon Redden for being such a wonderful friend and also for taking the time to proofread the manuscript. She has always been supportive of our family.

In addition, we owe a world of gratitude to our sisters, Myrtle, Violet, and Katie, who, along with our parents, taught us the skill of parenting. We know the most important ingredient to parenting is love, but their advice over the years has been invaluable. All three have been unconditionally supportive and available for consultation at a moment's notice. We also appreciate Mike Campion and Jim Fitzpatrick and couldn't imagine two more perfect "best men." We know their love and support made it possible for us to marry in California in 2008. We love you all, dearly.

We are overwhelmed with gratitude for the many friends and family members who have supported us through the years, and continue to do so. They have respected our relationship and treated us like any other family. Our journey would have been tiresome and thankless if not for their steadfast love and support.

And finally, we feel blessed to have been able to walk the path forged by so many before us, and we thank all the marriage equality plaintiffs and attorneys who dedicated so much of their time and efforts to change minds and hearts ... and laws.

~ BOBBI BUCHANAN ~

Much love and gratitude to our editor and publisher Wanda Fries for believing in this project and delivering it into the world.

Thank you also to David Buchanan, my first reader and number one cheerleader, and to my dear friend Kim Anderson for her careful reading and gentle fine-tuning of the manuscript.

I am forever indebted to all my family and friends for their constant support, inspiration, and creative energy, especially Cecilia, Mary, John, Cheryl, Jude, Rob, Erin, Austin, Becky, and Kim.

For understanding the importance of writing in my life and never complaining, I give my heartfelt thanks to my children, Aaron, Rachel, and Bryan, and my granddaughters, Chloe and Kylie.

Thank you most of all to Randy and Paul not only for bringing me on board, but for teaching me so much about love and family and standing up for one's self. Writing their story has made my life richer. I'm lucky to know them.